D1454549

PRELUDE TO OVERLORD

Dedicated to all those who took part in Operation *Overlord* and the subsequent liberation of Europe, whether in the air, on land or at sea.

Prelude to Overlord

An account of the air operations which preceded and supported Operation Overlord, the Allied landings in Normandy on D-Day, 6th of June 1944

Humphrey Wynn &
Susan Young

Airlife England

ISBN 0 906393 27 2

First published 1983
by Airlife Publishing Ltd.

Printed in England by Livesey Ltd., Shrewsbury.

Airlife Publishing Ltd.

7 St. John's Hill, Shrewsbury, England.

Contents

Authors' Note

Operation *Overlord* was the biggest combined operation the world had ever seen. Its aims were to transfer armies across the English Channel, to land them on a heavily defended French coast, to secure a military foothold in Normandy and from there to begin the liberation of Western Europe from Nazi Germany. It brought together the armed forces of many nations—those of Britain and of her European allies striving to regain their independence, of British Commonwealth countries and of the United States—and it assembled air forces, armies and navies in a massive interlocking of plans and activities; for no one arm could have succeeded without the others on D-day, June 6, 1944.

The air forces had a special role to play in establishing their superiority over the Luftwaffe long before the assault took place and in ensuring that much of the potential opposition to the Allied armies should be either neutralised or weakened. The air forces' role prior to, and at the time of, *Overlord* is the subject of this account. It takes as its starting-point the background to, reasons for and planning of the great operation; it does not pretend to be comprehensive or chronological, for to describe even the air aspects of *Overlord* in detail would require a very much bigger book than this one; indeed, most of the themes touched upon have themselves been the subjects of books.

What it does aim to do is to convey some idea of the vast scale of effort—in terms of men and materials, damage and casualties, skill and heroism—which went into the assault upon Europe that led to the liberation of her countries from German occupation.

The authors have been indebted to many books and records on different aspects of Operation *Overlord;* these have been listed in a bibliography, not only to acknowledge indebtedness but also to provide a useful reading-list for whose who wish to study aspects of the subject more deeply. Where passages have been quoted (by permission — as recorded in the following Acknowledgements) this is because they come either from accounts by leading participants in these great events, or from specialist studies of different aspects of them: they therefore help to give authenticity and vividness to the text; for no authors can claim to have original knowledge, and are heavily dependent on those who have preceded them.

Acknowledgements

Permission from the following publishers, authors and agents to quote from the books named is gratefully acknowledged: Her Majesty's Stationery Office: *The Strategic Air Offensive against Germany 1939-1945,* by Sir Charles Webster and Dr Noble Frankland; *Report by the Supreme Commander to the Combined Chiefs of Staff on the operations in Europe of the Allied Expeditionary Force 6 June 1944 to 8 May 1945,* by General Dwight D. Eisenhower; *Victory in the West Vol I The Battle of Normandy,* by Maj L. F. Ellis; *A Short Historical Account of No 83 Group during the period 1st April 1943 to the end of the war in Europe,* by Sqn Ldr D. R. Morgan, BA; *From Normandy to Hanover, 84 Group, Second TAF,* by J. Robinson; *Grand Strategy (Vol V),* by John Ehrman; and *SOE in France,* by M. R. D. Foot. A. D. Peters and Co: *Air Power in War,* by Lord Tedder. Maj-Gen Haywood S. Hansell, USAF (Ret), author of *The Air Plan that defeated Hitler.* Frederick Muller Ltd and the author: *The Luftwaffe: a History,* by John Killen. Duckworth and Co Ltd and the author: *The German Air Force,* by Wg Cdr Asher Lee. Victor Gollancz Ltd and Simon & Schuster Inc: *The Longest Day,* by Cornelius Ryan. Hutchinson Publishing Group Ltd: *Currahee! We Stand Alone!,* by Donald Burgett. The author: *Mission Completed,* by Air Chief Marshal Sir Basil Embry, GCB, KBE, DSO, DFC, AFC, RAF (Ret). William Kimber & Co Ltd and the author: *Aircraft versus Submarine,* by Alfred Price. B. T. Batsford Ltd: *Eisenhower as Military Commander,* by Maj-Gen E. K. G. Sixsmith. E. P. S. Lewin & Partners: *Against the Sun,* by Edward Lanchbery. Acknowledgment is also made to Air Vice-Marshal H. A. V. Hogan, CB, DFC, RAF (Ret), and to Air Chief Marshal Sir Edmund Hudleston, GCB, CBE, RAF (Ret), former AOCs of Nos 83 and 84 Groups respectively, for their agreement to quotation from the group histories. Other acknowledgements have been made as quotation occurs in the text.

The authors also wish to record their thanks to the following organisations and individuals for their assistance in the preparation of this book: Air Historical and Publications Clearance Branches, Ministry of Defence (Gp Capt E. B. Haslam and Mr J. Spottiswood, AHB, and Mr H. H. Edmunds, PCB); MOD Adastral Library (Mrs Valerie Brooke); Bundesarchivs, Militargeschichtliches Forschungsamt, Freiburg i Breisgau and Koblenz, West Germany; Office of Air Force History, HQ United States Air Force, Washington, DC, USA (Mr Max Rosenberg); Imperial War Museum Photographic Library (Mr E. Hine); Mr John P. Mills and Mr Glenn L. Fielding for photographic material; Public Record Office (Mr N. E. Evans); Flt Lt Alfred Price; Mr. L. A. Smith who drew the map and Mr P. W. Anderson who loaned documentary material; and Mr Philip J. R. Moyes and Mr Chaz Bowyer for the use of their photographs.

For any errors or misinterpretations which may have occurred the authors alone accept responsibility.

Introduction

By John W. R. Taylor, FRAeS, FRHistS*

Published nearly forty years after *Overlord,* the massive invasion which began the liberation of Europe in the Second World War, this book describes the deployment of Allied air power in the months preceding that operation.

June 6, 1944, was the day on which armies of men from Britain, the United States, Canada and their Allies crossed the narrow seas between England and France by ship and aircraft on what seemed to many expert observers to be a desperate gamble. True, the Germans had been driven from North Africa, and were being hard pressed in Italy and on the Russian front. But the Wehrmacht was far from beaten, and would clearly fight with courage and skill to keep the Allies out of the German homeland. The battle would be on territory it had overrun with almost contemptuous ease in the spring of 1940, and where it had repelled with grievous losses the Allied landing at Dieppe in 1942.

This is no mystery story with a suspenseful ending. No attempt has been made to set down stories of individual bravery, or even to divide the two opposing forces into "goodies" and "baddies" in the style of a Hollywood epic. *Overlord* was a grim battle that cost many thousands of lives. After almost four decades of reshuffled alliances, the question now whether the victims were British, American, German, French or any other nationality is a cause only for sadness that such a sacrifice should have been required. Yet no operation of war was ever more necessary.

The authors' objective has been to set down dispassionately and objectively the facts about the Allied air offensive prior to D-day. Orders of battle show the size of the air forces committed to battle on both sides, and tables of command their organisational structure; profiles of the opposing commanders give an insight into their experience and ability, which helped to determine the course of the air battles.

Notes on the types of aircraft available to those commanders are intended to emphasise their suitability for the tasks which lay ahead — in that environment at that particular time. Thus a fighter which achieved much in the heat and dust of North Africa, with primitive servicing and inadequate spares backing, might have proved too slow and cumbersome when matched against machines based on the sophisticated, well-equipped airfields of Europe; and the opponents in 1940s battles would find very different opposition over the beaches and hinterland of Normandy.

The authors describe the background to the pre-D-day offensive — the prelude to *Overlord* of their title — and from their account of the air fighting before that operation it becomes clear that the war was already lost for Nazi Germany. The final orgy of death and destruction that occupied the eleven months after June 6, 1944, could have been avoided as pointless for her and disastrous for the future wellbeing of the world, when her united adversaries would quickly become divided by a wall of suspicion and policies based on threats of mutual nuclear destruction.

*Editor, *Jane's All the World's Aircraft.*

Chapter 1

Background to Overlord

It was imperative for the Allies to re-enter Europe from the West if they were to win the Second World War: the Germans had to be defeated on land. Successful establishment of a foothold, however, required air superiority—as the Japanese had shown in Singapore in 1941-42. What happened when an invading force did not have any air support had been shown at Gallipoli in 1915; and despite extensive air cover the Dieppe operation in 1942 had been a costly exercise. The Americans fought their way across the Pacific because of growing air superiority in support of their island landings. When Operation *Torch*—precursor of *Overlord*—was successfully achieved on the North African coast in November 1942 the army was put ashore on territory that, if not necessarily friendly, was not openly hostile; though there was initial resistance from the Vichy French, a cease-fire was soon ordered. It was a different story when the Anglo-American forces, linking up with the 8th Army from the Western Desert, made their first landings in Europe—in Sicily and then at Salerno. On both those occasions, Allied air power was a crucial factor in eventual success.

Overlord, for which *Torch,* Sicily and Salerno—comprising an offensive against the "soft under-belly" of Europe—had been both grim dress rehearsals and an operational blooding, was to be the Western Allies' greatest test of the 1939-45 war. They could not afford to fail; and they could succeed only by controlling the air over the south of England, the Channel, the Normandy beaches and the areas to the east, west and south of them. This necessary control of the air had been assured initially by the Royal Air Force Fighter Command success in the Battle of Britain in 1940, the battle which followed the Franco-British defeat on land and the British withdrawal from Europe in May of that year. Had the RAF lost the Battle of Britain, the Germans would probably have put Operation *Sea Lion ('Seelöwe')* into effect. With control of the air over southern England, they might have done what no other European Power had succeeded in doing since the Normans in 1066—put an invading army ashore on the English coast.

In 1588 the Spaniards had wanted to transport their Netherlands army across the Channel, but their Armada was broken up by the English fleet. In 1805 the French army under Napoleon had been ready to sail across from Boulogne, but the Royal Navy had maintained its control of the sea through Nelson's victories. In 1940 the tide of war was running for the Germans; their Wehrmacht and its supporting Luftwaffe had proved victorious throughout Europe, from the Russian border to the North Sea; they were poised to avenge their 1918 defeat by a comprehensive victory in the west. But to make a successful landing on the south coast of England required control of the air over the Channel and southern Britain, and this had been denied to the Luftwaffe by RAF Fighter Command. By October 1940 the Battle of Britain had been decided: the Luftwaffe turned to a night bombing offensive for which it had never been designed. This victory in the second major battle of the 1939-45 War was the defensive cornerstone upon which the whole of the subsequent successful Allied offensive in Europe was built: hence its crucial relevance to the events of June 1944.

Had the RAF lost command of its native air in 1940, and had Britain then been invaded by the Germans and subjugated, four main consequences would have followed: the UK Government would have had to shift its seat, and its direction of the war, overseas; the U-boats would have roamed unchecked into the Atlantic; Bomber Command would have had to abandon the offensive it had waged against the German Reich since 1939; and, most important of all, the Americans—assuming that they had come into the war when they did — would not have had a European foothold to bring in first their bombers and then their fighters, their tactical air force and their armies to play a decisive part in the Allies' successful re-entry into Europe.

Because the integrity of Britain was maintained in 1940, a base was assured for operations in the Atlantic, the Mediterranean, the Far East and over Europe; RAF Bomber Command continued and increased its strategic offensive; Fighter Command added aggressive sweeps over the continent to its defensive duties; and the USAAF 8th Air Force applied its daylight precision bombing techniques to attacks on German industry, its escorting long-range fighters taking significant toll of Luftwaffe defensive fighter strength in the process.

Thus Allied air superiority, so crucial to the success of the Normandy landings, was gradually built up from 1940 onwards, by both fighters and bombers, with all main elements of the Allied air forces contributing to it.

Everything tended from 1940 on towards an eventual Allied re-entry into Europe: air power alone could not defeat the Germans, but it could make the difference between success and failure in the inevitable land battles. However, the struggle to achieve air superiority was a long and bitterly contested one. Lord Tedder, who as Air Chief Marshal Sir Arthur Tedder was Deputy Supreme Allied Commander and also the air commander, said after the war in his Lees Knowles Lectures on *Air Power in War,* delivered at Cambridge University in 1947:[1]

"The fight for air superiority is not a straightforward issue like a naval battle or land battle; it is not even a series of combats between fighters; it is frequently a highly complex operation which may involve any or all types of aircraft. It is a campaign rather than a battle, and there is no absolute finality to it so long as any enemy aircraft are operating. It may be very local and temporary, i.e. covering a specific operation, or it may be widespread and sustained as it was in the final phase of the war in Europe".

In Sicily, he commented, "one could not help wondering if, when the show-down came on D-day, we should find that we really had done the job. It would have needed only a small surviving enemy force to do immense damage during the initial landings. The fact that when D-day came we found the enemy air forces had been paralysed is a matter of

[1] Hodder & Stoughton, 1948

12

Overlorders: the Supreme Allied Commander, General Dwight D. Eisenhower, is in the centre; on his right the Deputy Supreme Commander, Air Chief Marshal Sir Arthur Tedder; on his left the C-in-C, Allied Expeditionary Air Force, Air Chief Marshal Sir Trafford Leigh-Mallory; and behind, Maj-Gen Butler

history. Their order of battle had given an entirely false impression of their true state.

"There was a similar element of the unknown prior to the landings in Normandy, in spite of the fact that since 1940 Allied superiority had gradually extended from the British coast, over the coastal sea routes, across to the shores of Europe and finally to some extent over parts of Europe itself. How unknown was the degree of air superiority we had attained is shown by the fact that prior to D-day it was estimated that the Luftwaffe would carry out between 600 and 700 sorties per day over the area of the landings; whereas in fact (except for sudden bursts of activity when up to 350 sorties were flown in a day) they were unable to maintain a daily average of more than 200".

So said the Allied air commander, speaking reflectively when the events of 1944 were already history: but what of the tasks which, in 1943, faced the planners of the great assault on Europe?

This enterprise could not be undertaken lightly or unadvisedly, despite pressure from the Soviet Union—fighting a desperate battle with the invading Germans—for the opening of a second front in 1942. There was no question, for the Western allies, of failure; but there was the question of when, and where, they would succeed. Not until 1943, with the defeat of the Axis forces in North Africa, the invasion of Sicily by a combined operation that became a prototype for the Normandy landings, and the bitter pursuit of the Germans up through Italy, were the Western leaders able to consider the realities of a re-entry into Europe.

Before the decision to mount Operation *Torch* (the landing by the British First Army and US 2nd Corps in north-west Africa, to link up with the Eighth Army advancing from Egypt), a cross-Channel assault in 1942 had been considered; but because of British insistence on the priority of *Torch,* the Americans agreed that the assault on Europe would be made in 1943. However, one of the decisions taken at the Churchill—Roosevelt conference at Casablanca in January of that year was that Sicily should be invaded once North Africa had been cleared of Axis forces, in order to maintain pressure on the enemy in the Mediterranean theatre. The consequence of this decision was that the projected date for landings in Western Europe would have to be put back to 1944.

In support of this plan the Casablanca conference also decided that a combined RAF Bomber Command—USAAF 8th Air Force strategic bomber offensive should be mounted, aimed specifically at the enemy's war-making capacity and at his morale: this offensive was code-named *Pointblank* and began in mid-1943. Further, forces were to continue to be assembled for an invasion of the Continent; and a combined Allied planning staff responsible to the Supreme Allied Commander-designate was to be set up under his Chief of Staff, Lt-Gen F. E. (later Sir Frederick) Morgan.[1] A directive received by him on April 26, 1943, declared: "Our object is to defeat the German fighting forces in north-west Europe". He was instructed not only to prepare outline plans for the assault, but also plans for "an elaborate camouflage and deception scheme" during the summer of 1943, with the idea of convincing the enemy that the invasion of his fortress was to take place during that year.

These huge tasks, not only of organising every aspect of the Allies' re-entry into Europe but also of convincing "feint" operations beforehand, were successfully achieved by a multi-national planning staff (COSSAC) before the Supreme Commander himself was appointed. One of its crucial decisions, particularly relevant to this study of air operations in support of the Allied landings, was the approval given in 1943 to the formation of an Allied Expeditionary Air Force (originally called the Air Striking Command), which will be referred to later.

It was at the next conference of Allied leaders—*Trident,* held in Washington in May 1943—that a target date was set for the landings in Europe: 1 May 1944. Troops and equipment were to be established in the UK as quickly as possible: the air forces were expected to have about 11,400 aircraft—including 632 transports for army airborne operations. It was at Washington that this great Allied assault was code-named *Overlord.*

During 1943, as a consquence of the directives from Casablanca and Washington and the setting of a target date for landing in Europe, the Allied expeditionary forces'

---

[1] COSSAC (Chief of Staff to the Supreme Allied Commander) was the title not only of the chief of staff himself but became a code name for the organisation he headed. See Sir Frederick Morgan's own fascinating account, *Overture to Overlord* (Hodder & Stoughton, 1950).

organisation took shape in the UK; further, the continuing air warfare in the west, which had never ceased since 1939, was given a new dimension and impetus by the preparatory phase of *Overlord*. Not only were RAF Bomber Command and the US 8th Air Force supporting the invasion plans under the *Pointblank* directive, but new aspects of tactical air co-operation with the Armies which were to make the cross-Channel assault were being worked out and put into effect.

The Germans, beaten in North Africa and the Mediterranean and fighting a stubborn rearguard action northwards through Italy, knew that the Allies would attempt a landing somewhere in north-west Europe but did not know where or when or in what strength it would occur. Allied air supremacy gave them few chances of reconnaissance. In a sense, however, their military problems were simpler. They were fighting a defensive battle in the air and within a year or so would be fighting a defensive one on the ground. They had been fortifying the Channel coast for over three years—any forces setting foot on it were going to have a brutal reception. German problems, by 1943, were more ones of survival: logistics, supply and communications. It was these problems which the Allies, largely through air power, had to make impossible of solution. Allied air problems prior to *Overlord* were more those of administration, planning, training, co-operation between RAF and USAAF commanders, and the build-up of sufficient strength to maintain supremacy until the time of the landings, despite the attrition of preparatory operations—the offensive fighter sweeps and the daily/nightly toll of unceasing bomber attacks. For Operation *Overlord* a whole new air force was created in the UK—the Allied Expeditionary Air Force, designed specifically to support and to carry into battle the Allied armies which were going into Europe. It had fighter, bomber, reconnaissance and transport aircraft, and drew its component parts from both the RAF and USAAF—from the former's Bomber and Fighter Commands and from the latter's 9th Air Force. Such a versatile and varied air force, built up for the biggest combined operation ever planned, had never before been seen and probably never will be again.

The significance of the AEAF was that it was the kind of air force the Luftwaffe had been in 1940 — designed for the direct support of an advancing land force. It had to be ready to project itself on to the Continent, to avoid the necessity of forming what had been a new, cumbersome Command overseas, as had been the case in 1940. It had to be a mobile air force, moving with the Armies; it had to be flexible, ready to respond at very short notice to demands for close air support. It was to do in Europe what the Desert Air Force had done in North Africa; and, as will be shown, it grew up and trained with the Army formations it was to support in their re-entry into, and advance across, the Continent.

Total Allied air strength, by formations, in mid-1943 and up to the time of the *Overlord* assault, consisted of the following: RAF Bomber Command, USAAF 8th Air Force in the UK and 15th AF[1] in Italy, all concerned with the strategic air offensive against Germany and with *Pointblank* in support of invasion plans; RAF Fighter Command, concerned with the air defence of Britain but being changed from a metropolitan into an offensive, tactical air force; the USAAF 9th Air Force in the UK, consisting of light and medium bombers, fighters and transports; RAF 38 and 46 Groups, whose function (with

[1]For an evocative account of 15th AF operations, less well publicised than those of Bomber Command and the 8th AF, see *The Sky is a Lonely Place,* by Louis Falstein (Rupert Hart-Davies, 1951).

the US IXth Troop Carrier Command) was to tow and lift the Army's airborne forces—glider troops and parachutists—into battle when D-day came; and RAF Coastal Command, among whose functions was the protection from U-boat attack of shipping which brought in the supplies and munitions and troops from the United States to build up *Overlord* logistic requirements, and—on D-day itself—protection of the Allied armada from the U-boats.

The Allied Expeditionary Air Force had as its RAF component, alongside the US 9th Air Force, the 2nd Tactical Air Force—created from Fighter Command and the light bomber formation (No 2 Group) of Bomber Command. It was officially formed on 1 June 1943, almost exactly a year before the Normandy landings it was designed to support. Its operations started with its creation, many months before the Anglo-American armies went ashore or dropped from the skies into Normandy[1].

It consisted originally of No 2 Group, transferred to it from Bomber Command and containing that command's light bombers—Mitchells, Bostons and Venturas (shortly withdrawn and replaced by Mosquito VIs); No 83 (Composite) Group, which had been formed on 1 April 1943 and by D-day had ten wings—a total of 29 squadrons (13 with Spitfires, ten with Typhoons and six with Mustangs); and No 84 Group, which, like No 83, had ten wings and 29 squadrons—15 with Spitfire IXs, eight with Typhoon 1Bs and three with Mustang IIIs, plus the three photo-reconnaissance squadrons of No 35 (Recce) Wing with Mustang 1As and Spitfire XIs. The Typhoons and Mustangs, armed with rockets, were perhaps the most devastating weapons in Allied hands for support of ground forces. The Germans, in their invasions of Poland in 1939, of France and the Low Countries in 1940 and of Russia in 1941, had never had air-to-ground armour of such potency. A fourth group, No 85 (Base) Group, was formed in December 1943 with the purely defensive task of providing air protection for the invasion build-up area in southern England, and for night coverage of 2nd TAF bases and Army units at the front once the landings had been made. By D-day its 12 squadrons were equipped with Mosquito XIIIs, Spitfire VIIs, IXs and XIVs, and Tempest Vs. There was also a second photo-reconnaissance wing in 2nd TAF; this was No 34 Recce Wing, which had three squadrons, equipped with Spitfire XIs, Mosquito IXs and XVIs, and Wellington IIIs. Additionally seven Fleet Air Arm units with Spitfire Vs, Seafire IIIs and Typhoons were attached to 2nd TAF and formed the Air Spotting Pool.

To complete the line-up of the British component of the Allied Expeditionary Air Force, there were two transport groups, Nos 38 and 46. These would tow and lift the gliders and paratroops of the British, Canadian and Polish airborne forces into battle, as vanguard of the Normandy landings. No 38 had ten squadrons—four with Albemarles, four with Stirlings and two with Halifaxes. No 46 had five squadrons of Dakotas.

Side by side with the RAF, RAAF, RCAF, RNZAF, Belgian, Czech, Dutch and Polish squadrons in 2nd TAF there was the American element of the Allied Expeditionary Air Force, the USAAF 9th Air Force.

This had been re-activated in the UK on 16 October 1943; its headquarters were at Sunninghill Park, Berks, and it was commanded by Lt-Gen Lewis H. Brereton, with Brig-Gen Victor H. Strahm as Chief of Staff. The main characteristic of the 9th AF was

[1]It was called 2nd TAF to differentiate it from the 1st and 3rd Tactical Air Forces, based respectively in the Mediterranean and SEAC (South-east Asia Command).

its versatility: it had 1,800 fighters, 400 light bombers, 800 medium bombers and 1,400 transports—a total of 4,400 aircraft of four different kinds; it also had five squadrons of photographic reconnaissance aircraft. The fighters were Lightnings, Mustangs and Thunderbolts (54 squadrons all told), plus four squadrons of Mustang tactical reconnaissance fighters. The light bombers were 12 squadrons of Havocs (Douglas A-20s); the medium bombers were 32 squadrons of Marauders (Martin B-26s) with one pathfinder squadron of Marauders. The transports were all Dakotas (Douglas C-47s and C-53s)—56 squadrons plus one pathfinder squadron. The five squadrons of reconnaissance aircraft in the 9th Air Force were equipped variously with Lightnings (Lockheed P-38s), Havocs and Black Widows (Northrop P-61s).

Although there was a clear distinction between the air forces which were to move on to the Continent with the *Overlord* armies (i.e. 2nd Tactical Air Force and the 9th US Air Force which together made up the Allied Expeditionary Air Force) and those which were to remain in the United Kingdom (i.e. the three RAF Commands—Fighter, Bomber and Coastal—and the 8th US Air Force), Bomber Command and the 8th AF were from May 1943 onwards playing a powerful part in preparations for D-day. Operating under the *Pointblank* directive, which was reaffirmed during the Teheran and Cairo conferences of November and December 1943 respectively, the strategic bomber forces were made responsible for the progressive destruction and dislocation of the German military, industrial and economic system, disruption of vital elements of lines of communication, and the material reduction of German air combat strength. These tasks, to be fulfilled by a successful prosecution of the combined bomber offensive, were considered to be a prerequisite of *Overlord*.

To accomplish them, the American and British bomber forces had the following strengths in 1943-44: 8th US Air Force, 2,788 heavy bombers (B-17 Flying Fortresses and B-24 Liberators) and 1,242 escort fighters (P-38 Lightnings, P-47 Thunderbolts and P-51 Mustangs); 15th US Air Force (based in Italy), 1,297 heavy bombers and 700 escort fighters; RAF Bomber Command, 1,408 heavy bombers (Avro Lancasters, Handley Page Halifaxes, Short Stirlings and DH Mosquitos.) With the USAAF attacking by day, the RAF made mainly night attacks—so the combined bomber offensive was a round-the-clock operation.

A special Bomber Command group, No 100, was formed on 23 November 1943; consisting of ten squadrons by mid-1944, its special task was to confound and destroy the enemy's defences. Two of its squadrons, Nos 214 and 199, equipped respectively with Fortresses and Stirlings, were joined on the eve of the Normandy landings by Fortresses of the USAAF 803rd Squadron to produce a *Mandrel* screen, to cover the invasion fleet. Jamming devices used were:

Jostle, a high-powered transmitter, employed against Luftwaffe fighter control frequencies; *Mandrel,* against the enemy's ground radar; and *Piperack,* against his airborne radar. As a defensive countermeasure, the strips of metal foil known as *Window* were dropped to simulate a bomber stream or even (as will be described later) a naval armada.

Another squadron, No 192, had an electronic countermeasures role, using Halifaxes, Wellingtons and Mosquitos over enemy coasts to detect signals from new radar devices. Additionally, fighter Mosquitos of Nos 23, 85, 141, 157, 169, 239 and 515 Squadrons kept up a war of attrition, with attacks on Germany's airborne defences, destroying on average three enemy aircraft each night through the use of *Serrate IV* and *Perfectos*. These radio countermeasures devices were, respectively, airborne equipment for homing RAF fighters on to Luftwaffe AI (airborne interception) transmissions and an airborne homer on its IFF (identification, friend or foe). No 515 was the first squadron in 100 Group to start low-level intruder attacks on enemy night-fighter bases, following the group's improvement in operating techniques and serviceability[1]. The three *Serrate*-equipped squadrons were Nos 141, 169 and 239.

The point to be made here is that the *Overlord* air operations with which this account is concerned cannot be isolated from the offensives being carried on by RAF and USAAF squadrons against Germany from the UK, although an entirely new air force, the Allied Expeditionary Air Force, was being set up to support the Normandy landings and the advance through Europe into the heart of Germany. No action in history can be dissociated from ones that have gone before, and this was particularly true of the air operations for a year preceding June 6, 1944. Strategic bombing, under the Combined Bomber Offensive directive, of January 21, 1943, approved by the Combined Chiefs of Staff at the Casablanca conference, was intended to be "a strategic preparation for *Overlord*", as *The Strategic Air Offensive against Germany 1939-1945*[2] puts it, adding: "It was intended to produce air superiority, a disruption of German military and industrial production and a decline in German morale, all of which were regarded as indispensable prerequisites to the successful military invasion of the Continent".

This was excellent in theory; a mighty bomber force (by the middle of 1944 the USAAF 8th and 15th Air Forces and RAF Bomber Command could together field more than 5,000 four-engined bombers against Germany and targets in her subject territories) combined with land, naval and supporting tactical air forces to mount the biggest assault ever made from the sea: how could it fail?

The problems on the Allied side were not ones of quantity: they had, in addition to the heavy bombers, tactical air forces numbering 2,840 fighters and fighter-bombers, plus 1,520 light and medium bombers (these including the most potent weapon of all for use against ground troops, the rocket-firing fighters). Against this air assault the German defensive strength on all fronts prior to the Normandy landings lay in the following categories and strengths: single-engined fighters: 1,523, of which 59 per cent were serviceable; night fighters: 778, of which 68 per cent were serviceable; twin-engined fighters: 242, of which 51 per cent were serviceable; and dive bombers and ground-attack aircraft: 1,005, of which 75 per cent were serviceable.

The chief Allied problem was that of leadership of the air power which was to precede, accompany and make possible the entry into Europe. One of the decisions which led eventually to the Normandy landings had been that taken at the Washington conference (code-named *Arcadia*) in December 1941—January 1942, when it was agreed that the Western Allies' war effort should be combined, that a CCS (Combined Chiefs of Staff) organisation should be set up, and that Germany was the prime enemy—and in her defeat lay the key to victory.

Initial planning for the landings (after the Casablanca conference in January 1943 had

[1]See *Mosquito,* by C. Martin Sharp and M. J. F. Bowyer; Faber and Faber, 1967.
[2]Sir Charles Webster and Dr Noble Frankland; HMSO 1961

decided that Sicily should be invaded first) began with a Combined Chiefs of Staff directive to the Chief of Staff to the Supreme Allied Commander (Designate), (COSSAC), Lt-Gen F. E. Morgan. Although having as yet no Supreme Allied Commander to whom to report, he was charged with the preparation of plans for three operations: (a) diversionary activities during 1943, designed to pin down the enemy in the west; (b) *Rankin,* which envisaged a return to the Continent in the event of German resistance disintegrating, at any time from April 1943 onwards; and (c) *Overlord,* an opposed landing in Europe during 1944.

In the event, there was no diversionary operation, no repetition of the costly Dieppe-type assault of 1942; and there was no *Rankin,* because German resistance showed no signs of disintegrating during 1943, despite reverses on the Russian front and in North Africa and the increasing weight of the Allied air offensive against the German home front.

But there was an *Overlord,* the air dimension of which forms the subject of this book, and one of the decisions which was taken as part of the planning for it was to set up a tactical air force. Because it was thought that the major role of an Allied Tactical Air Force was to give fighter cover over the beach-head, the commander of RAF Fighter Command (now called Air Defence of Great Britain), Air Chief Marshal Sir Trafford Leigh-Mallory, was appointed Commander-in-Chief, Allied Expeditionary Air Force, as a result of one of the decisions of the Quebec conference (code-named *Quadrant*) in August 1943.

This appointment would have caused no problems had air support for the Normandy landings been confined to fighters, ground-attack aircraft, medium bombers and troop transports; but there was a strong school of thought in favour of bringing in the strategic bomber forces as direct support for *Overlord.* However, the commanders of these forces, Air Chief Marshal Sir Arthur Harris (RAF Bomber Command) and Lt-Gen Carl "Tooey" Spaatz (Commanding General, US Strategic Air Forces in Europe, i.e. the 8th in the UK and the 15th in Italy), had equally strong ideas about the role of the heavy bombers and their ability to win wars by themselves[1].

In early 1943 the RAF and USAAF planned a combined bombing offensive which reflected the directive emanating from the Casablanca conference, that the purpose of the air war against Germany should be "to bring about the progressive destruction and dislocation of the German military, industrial and economic system and the undermining of the morale of the German people to a point where their capacity for armed resistance is fatally weakened".

Commenting on this directive in his book *The Air Plan That Defeated Hitler*[2] the former chairman and director of the planning team which planned the combined bomber offensive and Deputy Air Commander, Maj-Gen Haywood S. Hansell, Jr, USAF (Ret), said that it "in general ... prescribed the purpose of the air offensive against Germany.... The plans included the presumption that at the appropriate time the Strategic Air Forces would be temporarily used by the Supreme Commander, Allied Expeditionary Forces, in direct preparation for the invasion of the Continent, which was to be undertaken in the spring of 1944".

[1] In *Overture to Overlord* (page 102) Lt-Gen Sir Frederick Morgan (COSSAC) refers to "the problem of persuading the Bomber Barons to play with us in spite of the overriding demands of their private war over the Reich, at this time getting into its thunderous stride."
[2] Published in Atlanta, Georgia, 1972.

What Pointblank meant: the St Pierre des Corps marshalling yards at Tours, France, devastated after an attack by RAF Bomber Command aircraft on the night of April 10/11, 1944

Plans for the combined bomber offensive (code-named *Pointblank)* were presented to the Joint Chiefs of Staff in Washington on April 20, 1943, by General Ira C. Eaker, Commanding General of the US 8th Air Force; they were approved by the Combined Chiefs of Staff on May 18, 1943. However, as Maj-Gen Hansell points out:-

"Sometime between the presentation of the Plan for the combined bomber offensive … and its final adoption by the Combined Chiefs of Staff … a sentence was added to the Casablanca Directive which had far-reaching consequences." This sentence, coming at the end of the paragraph quoted above, said: "This is construed as meaning so weakened as to permit initiation of final combined operations on the Continent". The sentence, he considered, "was probably associated with another basic decision reached by the Combined Chiefs of Staff at this same meeting, i.e. … to invade France in the summer of 1944". It raised doubts as to the basic strategic purpose of the combined bomber offensive, and as a result, "three basic interpretations of the Casablanca Directive were now in evidence".

One of these was that of RAF Bomber Command, which (says Maj-Gen Hansell) considered "undermining of the morale of the German people" as the significant clause relating to the "point where their capacity for armed resistance is fatally weakened". A second was that of the US Strategic Air Forces, which looked on "the progressive destruction and dislocation of the German military, industrial and economic system" as the path to the "fatal weakening". Thirdly, however, "top-level soldiers and sailors of both nations—and to a large degree the President and Prime Minister as well—considered the primary purposes of the combined bomber offensive to be something quite different from that envisioned by the airmen. To them, the real objective of the bombing offensive was making possible an invasion of the Continent. In their view, the 'fatal weakening' meant the destruction and dislocation of the German military system which would ordinarily oppose the invasion. 'This is construed as meaning so weakened as to permit initiation of final combined operations on the Continent'.

Here Maj-Gen Hansell put his finger on the chief problem which faced the Allies in making their air plans for *Overlord*—the fact that there were two powerful strategic air forces engaged in day and night offensives against Germany; air forces with determined commanders (General Carl Spaatz and Air Chief Marshal Sir Arthur Harris) who believed that the bombing operations which they controlled could bring about the defeat of Germany without any land forces being involved.

As examples of this view, Maj-Gen Hansell may be quoted once more on the so-called "big week" (the last week of February 1944) and Air Chief Marshal Sir Arthur Harris, AOC-in-C, RAF Bomber Command, on the Battle of Berlin.

"In the last week of February 1944" (Maj-Gen Hansell writes) "the long-awaited opportunity to strike a lethal blow at the German Air Force finally arrived", and from February 20 onwards attacks were mounted by the Eighth, Ninth and Fifteenth US Air Forces and by RAF Bomber Command. "The back of the German Air Force was broken in February of 1944. The Allied Strategic Air Forces, with the assistance of the fighters of the Ninth (Tactical) Air Force, having defeated the German Air Force and attained the neutralisation of the 'intermediate' objective, were now ready to turn in force to the primary target systems. Unfortunately, it was late in the day .... Only three months remained before D-day, and much of the power of the air offensive would be diverted from the primary objectives of the combined bomber offensive and absorbed instead in operations intended to soften up the German ground forces and delay movements which directly threatened the Normandy beaches. This diversion of strategic air forces to short-term objectives was carried out at the insistence of General Eisenhower over the vigorous protest of General Spaatz".

That last sentence seems to sum up and typify the views of the bomber leaders that their offensives were all-important, that these could by themselves win the war and that anything else the strategic air forces were asked to do was merely a diversion. It also makes the point that it was only Eisenhower, as Supreme Allied Commander and an American, who could make the chief American bomber commander do what he wanted.

Exactly the same sort of problem faced the Royal Air Force in bringing in Bomber Command to support *Overlord* operations; for its AOC-in-C, Air Chief Marshal Sir Arthur Harris, was as dedicated in his opinions upon bomber capability as the commander of the United States Strategic Air Forces in Europe, General Carl Spaatz. Harris believed, for example, that the Battle of Berlin could win the war if it were continued and that it should go on until the "heart of Nazi Germany ceases to beat". He commented sarcastically in a memorandum of January 1944 that *Overlord* "must now presumably be regarded as an inescapable commitment". Nor was Harris prepared to take orders from Air Chief Marshal Sir Trafford Leigh-Mallory, Commander-in-Chief of the Allied Expeditionary Air Force, which was to provide tactical air support for *Overlord* operations. There were, in a word, serious national and command problems on the Allied side in addition to those of planning air support for the Normandy landings.

The authors of *The Strategic Air Offensive against Germany 1939-1945,*[1] Sir Charles

[1] HMSO, 1961

Webster and Dr Noble Frankland, summed up this watershed in the leadership and philosophy of Allied air power as its great floodtide was about to burst upon Europe in this way:-

"The sense in which these various problems (notably of priority between, and association of, *Pointblank* and *Overlord*) were eventually adjusted was of fundamental and lasting importance to the strategic air forces, which at this time were approaching the summit of their strength in numbers and of their effectiveness in striking power. This was not simply a question of another diversion like those which had occurred in the Battle of France, the Battle of the Atlantic and on other occasions. ... It was not only a question of aims and methods such as that which had arisen between the British and American Air Staffs and latterly between the Air Staff and Bomber Command. ... The arrangements made to ensure the success of *Overlord* and to maintain the subsequent land battle and the system of command by which they were executed transcended the earlier controversies of bombing strategy. ... They marked a transition for the heavy bombers from an offensive which ... had ... been primarily independent and strategic, to one in which their role was as an element in what the barbarous jargon of the time described as 'triphibious' war. Henceforth, the distinctions between 'independent' and 'auxiliary' and between 'strategic' and 'tactical' bombing became more and more confused. The wars in the air, on land and at sea became related to an extent which had been so only in theory at earlier stages and, in the process, the effectiveness of each arm gained immeasurable but undoubted strength".

But up till the early months of 1944 the leaders of both strategic air forces clung to their vew that Germany could be defeated by bombing her industry and destroying the morale of her civilian population. Yet, in the event, the most significant contributions of these offensives to the final chapter in the war were the attrition of the German fighter defences by the long-range fighters of the US 8th Air Force escorting its B-17s and B-24s, and the destruction of communications—canals, bridges and railways—in advance of the Allied armies and in rear of the retreating German Army. But this 'Transportation Plan', as it was called, was only put into effect through the authority and prestige of the Deputy Supreme Allied Commander—an airman, Air Chief Marshal Sir Arthur Tedder.

His appointment, which he took up with effect from January 20, 1944, was the last link in the command chain which was to weld the Allied air forces into an effective fighting arm; for from March 27 his post carried with it the overall direction of those air forces. He had been recommended as Deputy Supreme Commander by General Eisenhower, who had assumed the duties of Supreme Allied Commander on January 16, 1944. The two men had had a successful association in the Mediterranean theatre; both were diplomatic and skilful in their handling of subordinate commanders who might be truculent and fractious though skilful and successful. Their co-operation as Supreme Commander and Deputy, with the latter having authority for air operations, proved a triumphant solution to the problems of national loyalties, sensitiveness over seniority and dogged pursuit of policies at variance with the objectives of *Overlord.* Thus, while the US Air Force commanders were unwilling to accept orders from Air Chief Marshal Sir Trafford Leigh-Mallory as Allied Air Commander, *Overlord,* they would (as General Spaatz did) take them from Eisenhower or (as Air Chief Marshal Sir Arthur Harris did)

USAAF 15th Air Force operations from Italy:-

B-24s over the railway yards at Salzburg, Austria, smoke from the bombs they have just dropped mingling with that from enemy "smudge pots" on the ground

B-24s over the Alps, en route to targets in Austria. Against the snowy background, five B-24s can be seen from the photographic aircraft

B-17s (possibly of the 390th Bomb Group) encountering flak during a mission against German targets in France

A B-17 bearing a 306th Group 'H' on its fin, hit by flak and with part of its starboard wing on fire, releases its load – probably eight 500lb bombs – over Berlin. The two B-17s below have probably just released their bombs. Typical bomb load for that range was 4-5,000lb (e.g., ten 500lb or five 1,000lb bombs)

from Tedder. In the latter case, Tedder not only had the requisite status and rank, but proven command of air power in support of armies in the Western Desert and Sicilian campaigns.

In his post-war report on AEF operations[1] the position about control of the strategic bombing forces in the context of *Overlord* was explained quite simply by General Eisenhower, as follows:-

"By a decision taken by the Combined Chiefs of Staff, prior to my arrival in the Theater, command of the strategic bombing forces—the RAF Bomber Command and the United States Strategic Air Forces (composed of the Fifteenth Air Force in the Mediterranean Theater and the Eighth Air Force in the European Theater) — ultimately rested with the Combined Chiefs themselves. This decision had been taken with the purpose of co-ordinating strategic bombing against Germany from all sides. Within the European Theater overall command of the United States Strategic Air Forces rested with General (then Lieut-General) Carl A. Spaatz and command of the RAF Bomber Command with Air Chief Marshal Sir Arthur Harris. The Strategic Air Forces were thus not under my direct orders, their commanders being instead responsible directly to the Combined Chiefs in Washington. While understanding the long-range motives which brought this decision into being, I was nevertheless dissatisfied with the arrangement, feeling that, since responsibility for the principal effort against Germany fell upon my Headquarters, all the forces to be employed within the Theater—by land, sea and air—should be responsible to me and under my direction, at least during the critical periods preceding and succeeding the assault.

"I stated these views to the Combined Chiefs of Staff. At the same time I set forth the necessity for concentrated bombing of the rail network of Northwest Europe and particularly France, to which there was considerable opposition, the reasons for which will be considered shortly. I felt strongly about both these matters.

"In a review of the matter, the Combined Chiefs of Staff, who were aware of my problems, gave me operational control of the air forces from April 14. The Strategic Air Forces after this date were to attack German military, industrial and economic targets in an order of priority established within the Theater and approved by the Combined Chiefs. Additionally, they were to be available to me upon call for direct support of land and naval operations when needed. This was a role for which they had not previously been normally used, but the Salerno campaign had afforded convincing evidence of their effectiveness for the purpose.

"In the final command set-up of the air forces, then, the commanders of the Strategic Air Forces (RAF Bomber Command and the United States Strategic Air Forces) reported to Supreme Headquarters independently, as did also Air Chief Marshal Leigh-Mallory, commanding the tactical forces which comprised the Allied Expeditionary Air Force. The effort of the three separate commands was co-ordinated, under my direction, through the Deputy Supreme Commander, Air Chief Marshal Tedder".

After referring to the strategic air forces' assaults upon German aircraft production, oil supplies and communications, General Eisenhower added: "As the invasion date approached, a clear sign of our superiority in the air was the obvious unwillingness of the

[1]*Report by the Supreme Commander to the Combined Chiefs of Staff on the operation in Europe of the Allied Expeditionary Force June 6 1944 to May 8 1945*, HMSO, 1946.

25

enemy to accept the challenge to combat which we initiated with large-scale fighter sweeps over his territory. Our D-day experience was to convince us that the carefully laid plans of the German High Command to oppose *Overlord* with an efficient air force in great strength were completely frustrated by the strategic bombing operations. Without the overwhelming mastery of the air which we attained by that time our assault against the Continent would have been a most hazardous, if not impossible, undertaking."

So, on the Allied side, the stage was set by April 1944 for the dramatic re-entry into Europe and the leading actors in its air dimension had taken their places. Their opponents had been in position for nearly four years to meet the onslaught.

In what shape were these opponents, and what was likely to be the outcome of the air battles upon which victory in the West—and, in the end, the fate of Western Europe—would turn?

It is worth looking back briefly at the history of the Luftwaffe, now on the threshold of its last major conflicts and its final defeat. When the Second World War began it had been the most powerful air force in the world, advanced in equipment and high in morale. It had grown up with the resurgence of Germany under the Nazis, as an important part of the army, which it had been designed to support. During the Spanish civil war its Condor Legion had tried out equipment, techniques and crews on the Nationalist side, using that bitter internal conflict as a military research and development laboratory. A product of the Nazi determination to revive German military power, its needs were not subject to political debate and approval as were those of the air forces of the democratic countries. However, this could, and did, prove to be disadvantageous as well as an advantage; for the Luftwaffe was subject to political control, by Hitler through Göring, who was its first commander-in-chief (from 1935) and who later became the Air Minister (Reichsminister). This meant that Hitler's decisions, which could be disastrously wrong, like that in early 1944 to turn the Me262 jet fighters into fighter-bombers, had to be obeyed. Further, there was a reluctance on Göring's part, resulting from his old association with Hitler, to tell the Führer that there was anything wrong with his air force or anything that it could not do. Thus, though Hitler might ask for the impossible to be achieved—like the air supply of the German divisions trapped at Stalingrad, an operation which ended in failure for the Luftwaffe and defeat for the Wehrmacht—Göring was unwilling to tell him it could not be done, although the implications would be clear to the German air staff.

When the Luftwaffe faced the massed Allied air forces across the English Channel in early 1944, it had behind it a string of victories which had succeeded one another since 1938 and had not been interrupted until the Battle of Britain in 1940 and the reverses in Russia and North Africa in 1942. It had helped the Germany Army to overcome Austria, Czechoslovakia, Poland, France, Belgium, Holland, Denmark, Norway and Greece, to capture Crete from the air and to reach the gates of Egypt. But three things were not in its favour in the period before the Normandy landings: first, the Luftwaffe was principally an army air force, and its fortunes (apart from those in the air conflict for the defence of the German homeland against the Allied bomber offensive—a separate battle) ebbed and flowed with those of the Wehrmacht which it supported. Secondly, Luftwaffe successes had been gained when it was on the offensive with the Army; the Army was on the defensive in Northern France and a defensive battle is much harder to fight. Thirdly, in the campaigns which it had helped to win, the date and timing of the offensive had been chosen by the German High Command; but in the campaign which was to open in northern France the date and timing were being chosen by the Allies. When the blow fell, the Luftwaffe (in fact Luftflotte 3, commanded by Generalfeldmarschall Hugo Sperrle) would have to support whatever defensive operations the Wehrmacht mounted; and there was a fundamental division of opinion between the Army commanders, Rommel preferring to halt the Allies at the beaches and therefore making his defences as impregnable as possible there, von Runstedt opting for more fluid defensive tactics once the invading armies had gained their foothold in France.

Another problem for Sperrle was that his resources were not only limited (for reasons which became apparent after the war though weren't so evident at the time) but were not really of the right kind to stop invading forces which had considerable air superiority. Hitler's decision to convert the Me262 jet fighters to the fighter-bomber role, already mentioned, typified the dilemma. As fighters, these aircraft were faster than the P-51 Mustang; as fighter-bombers, they were probably no more effective than the FW190s. For the Germans, it was a question of priorities, and if Hitler as commander-in-chief decided upon a certain priority there was no gainsaying his decision.

But the Luftwaffe would have had to have hundreds of fighter-bombers, or hundreds of aircraft of the ground-attack calibre of the RAF Typhoons or USAAF P-47s, in order to have halted or turned back the Allied landings and subsequent advance into Normandy. Even, however, if they had possessed the requisite types of machine in sufficient numbers there would still have been the problems of shortage of experienced aircrew and—eventually—of fuel, although just before Operation *Overlord* started the Luftwaffe had adequate fuel reserves in northern France.

Despite the attrition on the Eastern front, and despite the defensive day-and-night battle against the strategic bomber offensive, the Luftwaffe still had plenty of aircraft in 1944. Thanks to the Armaments Minister, Albert Speer, and to the director of air armament, Generalfeldmarschall Erhard Milch, the German aircraft manufacturing industry turned out more machines in 1943 than it had in the previous year and gave the Luftwaffe an all-round superiority at the beginning of 1944, at least in numbers of aircraft. This was achieved by the large-scale employment of slave and foreign labour in the factories. But the emphasis was chiefly on fighters, and on types which had been in service since the beginning of the war.

New types which might have turned the tide of air war in Germany never got into large-scale production: the Me262, fastest fighter—next to the Me163—of the Second World War, has already been mentioned; in his book *The Luftwaffe: A History*[1] John Killen describes it as "perhaps the only new type ... that could have saved the Luftwaffe from defeat in 1945". The new four-engined bomber the He177 was a failure, although more than 1,000 were built; so was the Me210. Nevertheless, right up to 1945 the German aircraft industry was bringing out new types which, if they had been produced in numbers, might have had a decisive influence: the Me163 rocket fighter, though it was extremely limited in range and difficult to handle, and two other fighters, the Do335 and Ta152; new bombers like the Ju287 and the Arado 234. Some of them are described elsewhere in this book; the point here is that right up until the days of final defeat, German aviation engineers were still exercising extraordinary skill in their designs.

[1] Frederich Muller, 1967.

Amongst the most unusual of these were the two Heinkel He111s joined together to make one aircraft, and given a fifth engine; and the Ju88 plus Me109 combination known as *Mistletoe*, the manned fighter (on top) guiding the bomber which was loaded with explosives. In weapons, too, the Germans showed persistent ingenuity, gaining some success in 1943 and 1944 with the Henschel 293 glider bomber and *Fritz X* guided bomb, although these weapons could not be used effectively against Allied shipping concentrations before *Overlord*—partly because the Luftwaffe could not penetrate the UK fighter defences and partly because, owing to the failure of their reconnaissance (or the lack of it), they did not know where those concentrations were.

But in the Germans the Allies had a powerful and determined foe, as the air battles over the Reich proved; and the Luftwaffe launched counter-offensives both before and after the Normandy landings. The one before was a bomber attack on the UK, mounted from France in January 1944 and commanded by Generalmajor D. Peltz, nominated by Göring as Angriffsführer ("leader of the attack on") England. On the 21st, 447 bombers took off to raid London, 25 of them failing to return; on the 29th, a smaller force (285) repeated the operation and 18 were shot down; and the raids continued until the end of April, when the operation was discontinued because losses had become prohibitive. This was the last air "blitz" ever mounted by the Luftwaffe against Britain, but it was not the end of attacks on that country from the air. The worst was yet to come. The second counter-offensive, starting a week after the D-day landings—on June 13, 1944, was by unmanned vehicles, pilotless bombs (V-1s, or Vergeltungswaffe 1, Reprisal Weapon No 1) and subsequently by rockets (V-2s), which were launched continuously from September 8, 1944 until March 29, 1945.

However, the subject of this book is the Normandy landings by the Allies, and the German reaction in the period prior to and just after them. In assessing this an important factor to bear in mind is that the Luftwaffe, although entering upon what was to be the last chapter in its history, and although having been defeated both in North Africa and the Soviet Union, was still held in healthy respect by the Allies as a fighting force. Something of the reputation it had gained in 1940 with the all-conquering Wehrmacht—the Ju87/He111/Ju88 image of ruthless destruction created throughout Europe—still lingered; but by 1944 the Luftwaffe was suffering from the German army's widespread advances and conquests.

Quite apart from the great embroilment in Russia, which took more than a third of its total resources, the Luftwaffe had to spread its units in Western Europe from the north of Norway to the Atlantic coast of France and to Italy; and anywhere along the northern frontiers of territory held by the Third Reich an Allied landing (or landings) might come, though the Germans had no idea where or when. Thus, as Wg Cdr Asher Lee put it in his book *The German Air Force*,[1] "both the Luftwaffe and the Germany Army were compelled to divide their defensive resources and were never able to throw in the maximum shock forces immediately against the points of the Allied landing. The German military maxim of employing decisive forces at the decisive moment could find no practical expression in the air battles over the French battlefields in the summer of 1944. ..."

In the first nine months of the war, from September 1939 to June 1940, when the

[1]Duckworth, 1946.

German Army and the Luftwaffe had made all the running, they had chosen the times for their attacks and had made their main thrusts according to plan. They had held the initiative, but by 1944 the initiative was no longer with them but was passing to the Allies: having sown the wind in 1939/40 the Germans were now reaping the whirlwind.

The comment has already been made that the Luftwaffe in the West did not even have the right equipment in 1944 to repel an invasion backed by overwhelming air superiority. They would have needed several squadrons of fast reconnaissance aircraft (their speed giving them immunity from Allied fighters) with first-class photographic equipment; many squadrons of rocket-firing ground-attack machines which would have wrought havoc on the landing beaches; an equivalent number of fighter-bomber units, whose aircraft would have relied on fast low-level approaches and getaways; plus hundreds of tank-busting machines to slow down the Allied advance. But even if the Luftwaffe had had all these aircraft, their value would have been theoretical, since the Allied air forces were putting the German warning radars out of action, bombing airfields into uselessness and disrupting communications. Further, the French Resistance was making things extremely difficult for the German forces in northern France during the early months of 1944; and even if reinforcements were sent to the Luftwaffe facing the Allied landings, they might arrive too late or find themselves trying to land at bombed airfields. Of June 6, 1944, John Killen writes in his book *The Luftwaffe: A History,* already mentioned:-

"On this fateful day for Germany, von Sperrle, the commander of Luftflotte 3 in France, possessed only 300 operational aircraft, of which less than a hundred were fighters. In the event of invasion this small force—useless against anything more formidable than fighter-bomber attacks or similar sharp raids—was to be reinforced by the transfer of a further 600 aircraft from the Reich to prepared forward bases. Unfortunately, the order to move could only be given by Oberkommando der Luftwaffe headquarters; and the order came far too late. 'According to statements by its commanding general, Fliegerkorps II learned of the start of the invasion on June 6th at about eight o'clock in the morning,' writes Adolf Galland. 'Communications had been greatly disrupted and disorganised by the preceding air raids.' "

Accepting that the Luftwaffe was now on the defensive, that its resources were stretched, that its airfields were being bombed and its radars being put out of action, that it had lost many experienced aircrew and that the training programme was not producing adequate replacements, what was the actual situation of the Luftwaffe in northern France at the time of the Allied landings? Figures for the dispositions of Luftwaffe operational aircraft at 10 June 1944[1] show a strength of 1,300 (excluding transport types) in France and the Low Countries with 756 serviceable. Major components of this total were 475 single-engined fighters, with 290 serviceable; 464 bombers, with 267 serviceable; 170 night fighters, with 96 serviceable; and 46 twin-engined fighters, with 26 serviceable.

[1]Figures compiled from Quartermaster General Dept files, German AM.

Chapter 2

Allied Air Forces engaged in Overlord operations from the United Kingdom, 5 June 1944

Allied Expeditionary Air Force

RAF 2nd Tactical Air Force

No 2 GROUP

137 Wing:

88, 342 (Fr) Sqns	Hartford Bridge, Hants	Boston IIIA
226 Sqn	Hartford Bridge, Hants	Mitchell II

138 Wing:

107, 305 (Pol), 613 Sqns	Lasham, Hants	Mosquito VI

139 Wing:

98, 180, 320 (Dutch) Sqns	Dunsfold, Surrey	Mitchell II

140 Wing:

21, 464 (RAAF), 487 (RNZAF) Sqns	Gravesend, Kent	Mosquito VI

No 83 GROUP

39 (RCAF) Reconnaissance Wing:

400 (RCAF) Sqn	Odiham, Hants	Spitfire XI
168, 414 (RCAF), 430 (RCAF) Sqns	Odiham, Hants	Mustang I

121 Wing:

174, 175, 245 Sqns	Holmsley South, Hants	Typhoon IB

122 Wing:

19, 65, 122 Sqns	Funtington, Sussex	Mustang III

124 Wing:

181, 182, 247 Sqns	Hurn, Hants	Typhoon IB

125 Wing:

132, 453 (RAAF), 602 Sqns	Ford, Sussex	Spitfire IX

126 Wing:

401 (RCAF), 411 (RCAF), 412 (RCAF) Sqns	Tangmere, Sussex	Spitfire IX

127 Wing:

403 (RCAF), 416 (RCAF), 421 (RCAF) Sqns	Tangmere, Sussex	Spitfire IX

129 Wing:

184 Sqn	West Hampnett, Sussex	Typhoon IB

143 Wing:

438 (RCAF), 439 (RCAF), 440 (RCAF) Sqns	Hurn, Hants	Typhoon IB

144 Wing:

441 (RCAF), 442 (RCAF), 443 (RCAF) Sqns	Ford, Sussex	Spitfire IX

Air Observation Posts:

652 Sqn	Cobham, Surrey	Auster IV
653 Sqn	Penshurst, Kent	Auster IV
658 Sqn	Collyweston, Northants	Auster IV
659 Sqn	East Grinstead, Sussex	Auster IV
662 Sqn	Westley, Suffolk	Auster IV

No 84 GROUP

35 Reconnaissance Wing:

2, 268 Sqns	Gatwick, Surrey	Mustang IA
4 Sqn	Gatwick, Surrey	Spitfire XI

123 Wing:

198, 609 Sqns	Thorney Island, Sussex	Typhoon IB

131 Wing:

302 (Pol), 308 (Pol), 317 (Pol) Sqns	Chailey, Sussex	Spitfire IX

132 Wing:

66, 331 (Nor), 332 (Nor) Sqns	Bognor, Sussex	Spitfire IX

de Havilland Mosquito FB VI of the 2nd Tactical Air Force, bomb doors still open, after a low-level attack on Gael airfield

133 Wing:		
129, 306 (Pol), 315 (Pol) Sqns	Coolham, Sussex	Mustang III
134 Wing:		
310 (Cz), 312 (Cz), 313 (Cz) Sqns	Appledram, Sussex	Spitfire IX
135 Wing:		
222, 349 (Belg), 485 (RNZAF) Sqns	Selsey, Sussex	Spitfire IX
136 Wing:		
164, 183 Sqns	Thorney Island, Sussex	Typhoon IB
145 Wing:		
329 (Fr), 340 (Fr), 341 (Fr) Sqns	Merston, Sussex	Spitfire IX
146 *Wing:*		
193, 197, 257, 266 Sqns	Needs Oar Point, Hants	Typhoon IB
Air Observation Posts:		
660 Sqn	Westenhangar, Kent (ALG)	Auster IV
661 Sqn	Fairchilds, Kent (ALG)	Auster IV

No 85 (BASE) GROUP

141 Wing:

91 Sqn	West Malling, Kent	Spitfire XIV
124 Sqn	Bradwell Bay, Essex	Spitfire VII
322 (Dutch) Sqn	Hartford Bridge, Hants	Spitfire XIV

142 Wing:

264 Sqn	Hartford Bridge, Hants	Mosquito XIII
604 Sqn	Hurn, Hants	Mosquito XIII

147 Wing:

29 Sqn	West Malling, Kent	Mosquito XIII

148 Wing:

409 (RCAF) Sqn	West Malling, Kent	Mosquito XIII

149 Wing:

410 (RCAF) Sqn	Hunsdon, Herts	Mosquito XIII
488 (RNZAF) Sqn	Zeals, Wilts	Mosquito XIII

150 Wing:

56 Sqn	Newchurch, Kent	Spitfire IX
3, 486 (RNZAF) Sqns	Newchurch, Kent	Tempest V

34 Reconnaissance Wing:

16 Sqn	Northolt, Middlesex	Spitfire XI
140 Sqn	Northolt, Middlesex	Mosquito IX/XVI
69 Sqn	Northolt, Middlesex	Wellington XIII

Air Spotting Pool

26, 63 Sqns	Lee-on-Solent, Hants	Spitfire V
808 (FAA), 897 (FAA) Sqns	Lee-on-Solent, Hants	Seafire III
885 (FAA), 886 (FAA) Sqns	Lee-on-Solent, Hants	Seafire III
1320 Special Duty Flight	Lee-on-Solent, Hants	Typhoon

AIRBORNE AND TRANSPORT FORCES

No 38 Group

295, 570 Sqns	Harwell, Berks	Albemarle/Horsa
296, 297 Sqns	Brize Norton, Oxford	Albemarle/Horsa
190, 620 Sqns	Fairford, Glos	Stirling IV/Horsa
196, 299 Sqns	Keevil, Wilts	Stirling IV/Horsa
298, 644 Sqns	Tarrant Rushton, Dorset	Halifax V/Horsa/Hamilcar

No 46 Group

48, 271 Sqns	Down Ampney, Glos	Dakota/Horsa
233 Sqn	Blakehill Farm, Wilts	Dakota/Horsa
512, 575 Sqns	Broadwell, Glos	Dakota/Horsa

United States Ninth Air Force

10 Photographic Reconnaissance Group	Chalgrove, Bucks	Lightning, Havoc, Black Widow

IX TACTICAL AIR COMMAND

70 Fighter Wing:

48 Group	Ibsley, Hants	P-47 Thunderbolt
367 Group	Stoney Cross, Hants	P-38 Lightning
371 Group	Bisterne Close, Hants	P-47 Thunderbolt
474 Group	Moreton, Essex	P-38 Lightning

71 Fighter Wing:

366 Group	Thruxton, Hants	P-47 Thunderbolt
368 Group	Chilbolton, Hants	P-47 Thunderbolt
370 Group	Andover, Hants	P-38 Lightning

84 Fighter Wing:

50 Group	Lymington, Hants	P-38 Lightning
365 Group	Beaulieu, Hants	P-47 Thunderbolt
404 Group	Winkton, Hants	P-47 Thunderbolt
405 Group	Christchurch, Hants	P-47 Thunderbolt
67 Tactical Reconnaissance Group	Middle Wallop, Hants	F-6 Mustang

XIX TACTICAL AIR COMMAND

100 Fighter Wing:

354 Group	Lashenden, Kent	P-51 Mustang
358 Group	High Haldon, Kent	P-47 Thunderbolt
362 Group	Headcorn, Kent	P-47 Thunderbolt
363 Group	Staplehurst, Kent	P-51 Mustang

303 Fighter Wing:

36 Group	Kingsnorth, Kent	P-47 Thunderbolt
373 Group	Woodchurch, Kent	P-47 Thunderbolt
406 Group	Ashford, Kent	P-47 Thunderbolt

IX BOMBER COMMAND

97 Combat Bombardment Wing:

409 Group	Little Walden, Essex	A-20 Havoc
410 Group	Gosfield, Essex	A-20 Havoc
416 Group	Wethersfield, Essex	A-20 Havoc

98 Combat Bombardment Wing:

323 Group	Colne, Hunts	B-26 Marauder
387 Group	Stoney Cross, Hants	B-26 Marauder
394 Group	Boreham, Essex	B-26 Marauder
397 Group	Rivenhall, Essex	B-26 Marauder

Part of the preparatory air offensive before Overlord: an attack by B-26 Marauders of the USAAF 9th Air Force on the railway marshalling yards at Namur, Belgium, on April 10, 1944

A P-47 of the 354th Group, XIX Tactical Air Command, taxies in at Lashenden with groundcrewman on the port wing. Note the four 0.5in gun ports in the wing, the under-wing mountings for bombs and overload tank, the insignia and the victory crosses

99 Combat Bombardment Wing:

322 Group	Great Saling, Essex	B-26 Marauder
344 Group	Standstead Mountfitchet, Essex	B-26 Marauder
386 Group	Great Dunmow, Essex	B-26 Marauder
391 Group	Matching, Essex	B-26 Marauder
One Pathfinder Sqn		B-26 Marauder

IX TROOP CARRIER COMMAND

50 Troop Carrier Wing:

439 Group	Upottery, Devon	C-47 Skytrain*
440 Group	Exeter, Devon	C-47 Skytrain*
441 Group	Merryfield, Somerset	C-47 Skytrain*
442 Group	Weston Zoyland, Somerset	C-47 Skytrain* and C-53 Skytrooper†

*Known as Dakota I in Britain
†Known as Dakota II in Britain

52 Troop Carrier Wing:

61 Group	Barkston Heath, Lincs	C-47 and C-53
313 Group	Folkingham, Lincs	C-47 and C-53
314 Group	Saltby, Leics	C-47 and C-53
315 Group	Spanhoe, Northants	C-47 and C-53
316 Group	Cottesmore, Rutland	C-47 and C-53

53 Troop Carrier Wing:

434 Group	Aldermaston, Berks	C-47
435 Group	Welford, Berks	C-47 and C-53
436 Group	Membury, Berks	C-47
437 Group	Ramsbury, Wilts	C-47
438 Group	Greenham Common, Berks	C-47
One Pathfinder Group		Dakota

In addition, Troop Carrier Command used CG-4A and Horsa gliders.

RAF Air Defence of Great Britain

No 10 Group:

1,165 Sqns	Predannack, Cornwall	Spitfire IX
151 Sqn	Predannack, Cornwall	Mosquito XIII
41 Sqn	Bolt Head, Devon	Spitfire

'B' Flight, 276 Sqn (A/SR)	Bolt Head, Devon	Spitfire, Warwick, Walrus
126 Sqn	Culmhead, Somerset	Spitfire IX
131, 616 Sqns	Culmhead, Somerset	Spitfire VII
263 Sqn	Harrowbeer, Devon	Typhoon IB
610 Sqn	Harrowbeer, Devon	Spitfire XIV
68 Sqn	Fairwood Common, Glos	Beaufighter VIF
406 (RCAF) Sqn	Winkleigh, Devon	Beaufighter VIF Mosquito XII
1449 Flight	St Mary's, Scillies	Hurricane IIB

No 11 Group:

33, 74, 127 Sqns	Lympne, Kent	Spitfire IX
64, 234, 611 Sqns	Deanland, Sussex	Spitfire VB
80, 229, 274 Sqns	Detling, Kent	Spitfire IX
130, 303 (Pol), 402 (RCAF) Sqns	Horne, Surrey	Spitfire VB
345 (Fr) Sqn	Shoreham, Sussex	Spitfire
'A' Flight 277 Sqn	Shoreham, Sussex	Spitfire, Sea Otter, Walrus
350 (Belg) Sqn	Friston, Sussex	Spitfire VB
501 Sqn	Friston, Sussex	Spitfire IX
137 Sqn	Manston, Kent	Typhoon IB
605 Sqn	Manston, Kent	Mosquito VI
96 Sqn	West Malling, Kent	Mosquito XIII
125 (Newfoundland) Sqn	Hurn, Hants	Mosquito XVII
219 Sqn	Bradwell Bay, Essex	Mosquito XVIII
'A' Flight 278 Sqn	Bradwell Bay, Essex	Warwick
456 (RAAF) Sqn	Ford, Sussex	Mosquito XVII
418 (RCAF) Sqn	Holmsley South, Hants	Mosquito VI
275 Sqn	Warmwell, Dorset	Spitfire, Walrus
'B' Flight 277 Sqn	Hawkinge, Kent	Walrus, Spitfire
'B' Flight 278 Sqn	Martlesham Heath, Suffolk	Walrus, Spitfire

No 12 Group:

'A' Flight 504 Sqn	Digby, Lincs	Spitfire VB
316 (Pol) Sqn	Coltishall, Norfolk	Mustang III
'B' Flight 504 Sqn	Coltishall, Norfolk	Spitfire VB
25 Sqn	Coltishall, Norfolk	Mosquito XVII
307 (Pol) Sqn	Church Fenton, Yorks	Mosquito XII
Fighter Interception Unit	Wittering, Northants	Beaufighter, Mosquito, Mustang, Tempest

No 13 Group:

'A' Flight 118 Sqn	Sumburgh, Shetlands	Spitfire VB
'B' Flight 118 Sqn	Skeabrae, Orkneys	Spitfire VB
309 (Pol) Sqn	Drem, East Lothian	Hurricane IIC

Allied Strategic Air Force

RAF Bomber Command

No 1 Group:

12, 626 Sqns	Wickenby, Lincs	Lancaster I/III
100 Sqn	Grimsby, Lincs	Lancaster I/III
101 Sqn	Ludford Magna, Lincs	Lancaster I/III
103, 576 Sqns	Elsham Wolds, Lincs	Lancaster I/III
166 Sqn	Kirmington, Lincs	Lancaster I/III
300 (Pol) Sqn	Faldingworth, Lincs	Lancaster I/III
460 (RAAF) Sqn	Binbrook, Lincs	Lancaster I/III
550 Sqn	North Killingholme, Lincs	Lancaster I/III
625 Sqn	Kelstern, Lincs	Lancaster I/III

No 3 Group:

15, 622 Sqns	Mildenhall, Suffolk	Lancaster I/III
75 (RNZAF) Sqn	Mepal, Cambs	Lancaster I/III
115 Sqn	Witchford, Cambs	Lancaster I/III
514 Sqn	Waterbeach, Cambs	Lancaster II
90 Sqn	Tuddenham, Suffolk	Stirling III / Lancaster I/III
149 Sqn	Methwold, Norfolk	Stirling III
218 Sqn	Woolfox Lodge, Rutland	Stirling III
138 (Special Duty) Sqn	Tempsford, Beds	Halifax, Stirling
161 (Special Duty) Sqn	Tempsford, Beds	Hudson, Lysander, Halifax

No 4 Group:

10 Sqn	Melbourne, Yorks	Halifax III
51 Sqn	Snaith, Yorks	Halifax III
76 Sqn	Holme-on-Spalding-Moor, Yorks	Halifax III
77 Sqn	Full Sutton, Yorks	Halifax III
78 Sqn	Breighton, Yorks	Halifax III
102 Sqn	Pocklington, Yorks	Halifax III
158 Sqn	Lissett, Yorks	Halifax III
346 (Fr) Sqn	Elvington, Yorks	Halifax V/III
466 (RAAF) Sqn	Driffield, Yorks	Halifax III
578 Sqn	Burn, Yorks	Halifax III
640 Sqn	Leconfield, Yorks	Halifax III

No 5 Group:

9 Sqn	Bardney, Lincs	Lancaster I/III
44 (Rhodesian), 691 Sqns	Dunholme Lodge, Lincs	Lancaster I/III
49 Sqn	Fiskerton, Lincs	Lancaster I/III

Lancaster IIs (Hercules-engined, unlike the more familiar Merlin-engined version) lining up for take-off at one of the Yorkshire airfields of No 6 (RCAF) Group of Bomber Command

Lancaster IIIs of No 619 Sqn en route over stratus cloud. The leading aircraft was subsequently destroyed in a crash-landing and fire at Woodbridge when it returned from the Nuremberg raid of 30-31 March 1944 with two engines out of action

Lancaster I of No 156 Sqn, one of the original squadrons in No 8 (Pathfinder Force) Group. This squadron operated Lancaster Is and IIIs from January 1943 to the end of the war in Europe

A Halifax II Series I (Special) of No 77 Sqn, which operated this mark until May 1944. Later Halifaxes had rectangular fins

Halifax in daylight, in formation over friendly territory. This one, a Mk II Series IA, was from No 78 Sqn, which operated this mark until January 1944

50, 61 Sqns	Skellingthorpe, Lincs	Lancaster I/III
57, 630 Sqns	East Kirkby, Lincs	Lancaster I/III
106 Sqn	Metheringham, Lincs	Lancaster I/III
207 Sqns	Spilsby, Lincs	Lancaster I/III
463 (RAAF), 467 (RAAF) Sqns	Waddington, Lincs	Lancaster I/III
97, 83 Sqns	Coningsby, Lincs	Lancaster I/III
617 Sqn	Woodhall Spa, Lincs	Lancaster I/III Mosquito IV
627 Sqn	Woodhall Spa, Lincs	Mosquito IV

No 6 Group:

408 (RCAF) Sqn	Linton-on-Ouse, Yorks	Lancaster II
419 (RCAF) Sqn	Middleton St George, Durham	Lancaster X
428 (RCAF) Sqn	Middleton St George, Durham	Halifax II, Lancaster X
420 (RCAF), 425 (RCAF) Sqns	Tholthorpe, Yorks	Halifax III
424 (RCAF), 433 (RCAF) Sqns	Skipton-on-Swale, Yorks	Halifax III
426 (RCAF) Sqn	Linton-on-Ouse, Yorks	Halifax III
427 (RCAF), 429 (RCAF) Sqns	Leeming, Yorks	Halifax III
431 (RCAF), 434 (RCAF) Sqns	Croft, Yorks	Halifax III
432 (RCAF) Sqn	East Moor, Yorks	Halifax III/VII

No 8 Pathfinder Group:

7 Sqn	Oakington, Cambs	Lancaster I/III
35 Sqn	Graveley, Hunts	Lancaster I/III
156 Sqn	Upwood, Hunts	Lancaster I/III
405 (RCAF) Sqn	Gransden Lodge, Hunts	Lancaster I/III
582 Sqn	Little Staughton, Hunts	Lancaster I/III
635 Sqn	Downham Market, Norfolk	Lancaster I/III
105 Sqn	Bourn, Cambs	Mosquito IX
109 Sqn	Little Staughton, Hunts	Mosquito IX/XVI
139 Sqn	Upwood, Hunts	Mosquito
571 Sqn	Oakington, Cambs	Mosquito XVI
692 Sqn	Graveley, Hunts	Mosquito IV/XVI

No 100 (BS) Group:

85 (BS) Sqn	Swannington, Norfolk	Mosquito XIX
141 (BS), 239 (BS) Sqns	West Raynham, Norfolk	Mosquito VI
157 (BS) Sqn	Swannington, Norfolk	Mosquito XVII
169 (BS) Sqn	Great Massingham, Norfolk	Mosquito II
23 (BS), 515 (BS) Sqns	Little Snoring, Norfolk	Mosquito VI
214 (BS) Sqn	Oulton, Norfolk	Fortress II, III

192 (BS) Sqn	Foulsham, Norfolk	Wellington X, Halifax III, Mosquito IV
199 Sqn	North Creake, Norfolk	Stirling III
223 Sqn	Oulton, Norfolk	B-24 Liberator BVI

United States Eighth Air Force

7 Photographic Reconnaissance Group	Mount Farm, Bucks	Lightning, Spitfire

1st Bombardment Division

1st Combat Bombardment Wing:

91 Group	Bassingbourn, Cambs	B-17 Fortress
381 Group	Ridgewell, Essex	B-17 Fortress
398 Group	Nuthamstead, Herts	B-17 Fortress

40th Combat Bombardment Wing:

92 Group	Podington, Beds	B-17 Fortress
305 Group	Chelveston, Northants	B-17 Fortress
306 Group	Thurleigh, Beds	B-17 Fortress

41st Combat Bombardment Wing:

303 Group	Molesworth, Hunts	B-17 Fortress
379 Group	Kimbolton, Hunts	B-17 Fortress
384 Group	Grafton Underwood, Northants	B-17 Fortress

94th Combat Bombardment Wing:

351 Group	Polebrook, Northants	B-17 Fortress
401 Group	Deenethorpe, Northants	B-17 Fortress
457 Group	Glatton, Hunts	B-17 Fortress

2nd Bombardment Division

2nd Combat Bombardment Wing:

389 Group	Hethel, Norfolk	B-24 Liberator
445 Group	Tibenham, Norfolk	B-24 Liberator
453 Group	Old Buckenham, Norfolk	B-24 Liberator

14th Combat Bombardment Wing:

44 Group	Shipdham, Norfolk	B-24 Liberator
392 Group	Wendling, Norfolk	B-24 Liberator
492 Group	North Pickenham, Norfolk	B-24 Liberator

B-17s of the 92nd Bomb Group setting out on a mission

B-24s of the 446th Bomb Group en route to attack the German aircraft assembly plant and the transport centre at Bourges, south-east of Orleans, on 10 April 1944

20th Combat Bombardment Wing:

93 Group	Hardwick, Norfolk	B-24 Liberator
446 Group	Flixton, Suffolk	B-24 Liberator
448 Group	Seething, Norfolk	B-24 Liberator

95th Combat Bombardment Wing:

489 Group	Halesworth, Suffolk	B-24 Liberator
491 Group	Metfield, Suffolk	B-24 Liberator

96th Combat Bombardment Wing:

458 Group	Horsham St Faith, Norfolk	B-24 Liberator
466 Group	Attlebridge, Norfolk	B-24 Liberator
467 Group	Rackheath, Norfolk	B-24 Liberator

3rd Bombardment Division

4th Combat Bombardment Wing:

94 Group	Bury St Edmunds, Suffolk	B-17 Fortress
385 Group	Great Ashfield, Suffolk	B-17 Fortress
447 Group	Rattlesden, Suffolk	B-17 Fortress

13th Combat Bombardment Wing:

95 Group	Horsham, Suffolk	B-17 Fortress
100 Group	Thorpe Abbots, Norfolk	B-17 Fortress
390 Group	Framlingham, Suffolk	B-17 Fortress

45th Combat Bombardment Wing:

96 Group	Snetterton Heath, Norfolk	B-17 Fortress
388 Group	Knettishall, Suffolk	B-17 Fortress
452 Group	Deopham Green, Norfolk	B-17 Fortress

92nd Combat Bombardment Wing:

486 Group	Sudbury, Suffolk	B-24 Liberator
487 Group	Lavenham, Suffolk	B-24 Liberator

93rd Combat Bombardment Wing:

34 Group	Mendlesham, Suffolk	B-24 Liberator
490 Group	Eye, Suffolk	B-24 Liberator
493 Group	Debach, Suffolk	B-24 Liberator

VIII Fighter Command

65th Fighter Wing:

4 Group	Debden, Essex	P-51 Mustang
56 Group	Boxted, Essex	P-47 Thunderbolt
355 Group	Steeple Morden, Essex	P-51 Mustang

356 Group	Martlesham, Suffolk	P-47 Thunderbolt
479 Group	Wattisham, Suffolk	P-38 Lightning

66th Fighter Wing:

55 Group	Wormingford, Essex	P-38 Lightning
78 Group	Duxford, Cambs	P-47 Thunderbolt
339 Group	Fowlmere, Cambs	P-51 Mustang
353 Group	Raydon, Suffolk	P-47 Thunderbolt
357 Group	Leiston, Suffolk	P-51 Mustang

67th Fighter Wing:

20 Group	Kings Cliffe, Northants	P-38 Lightning
352 Group	Bodney, Norfolk	P-51 Mustang
359 Group	East Wretham, Norfolk	P-51 Mustang
361 Group	Bottisham, Cambs	P-51 Mustang
364 Group	Honington, Suffolk	P-38 Lightning

RAF Coastal Command

No 15 Group:

59, 120 Sqns	Ballykelly, Londonderry	Liberator V
422 (RCAF),	Castle Archdale,	Sunderland III
423 (RCAF) Sqns	Fermanagh	
811 (FAA) Sqn	Limavady	Swordfish, Wild Cat

No 16 Group:

143 Sqn	Manston, Kent	Beaufighter X
848 (FAA) Sqn	Manston, Kent	Avenger
819 (FAA) Sqn	Manston, Kent	Swordfish
236, 254 Sqns	North Coates, Lincs	Beaufighter X
455 (RAAF),	Langham, Norfolk	Beaufighter X
489 (RNZAF) Sqns		
Part 415 (RCAF) Sqn	Bircham Newton, Norfolk	Wellington XIII
854 (FAA), 855 (FAA) Sqns	Hawkinge, Kent	Avenger

No 18 Group:

86 Sqn	Tain, Ross and Cromarty	Liberator
210 Sqn	Sullom Voe, Shetlands	Catalina IV
330 (Nor) Sqn	Sullom Voe, Shetlands	Sunderland III
Part 333 (Nor) Sqn	Sumburgh, Shetlands	Mosquito
Part 333 (Nor) Sqn	Leuchars, Fifeshire	Mosquito VI
Part 333 (Nor) Sqn	Woodhaven, Fifeshire	Catalina IB
1693 Flight	Skitten, Caithness	Anson

No 19 Group

144, 404 (RCAF) Sqns	Davidstowe Moor, Cornwall	Beaufighter X
235 Sqn	Portreath, Cornwall	Beaufighter X
248 Sqn	Portreath, Cornwall	Mosquito VI
58, 502 Sqns	St Davids, Pembs	Halifax II
53, 224, 547 Sqns	St Eval, Cornwall	Liberator V
206 Sqn	St Eval, Cornwall	Liberator VI
311 (Cz) Sqn	Predannack, Cornwall	Liberator V
179 Sqn	Predannack, Cornwall	Wellington XIV
10 (RAAF) Sqn	Mount Batten, Devon	Sunderland III
201, 228, 461 (RAAF) Sqns	Pembroke Dock, Pembs	Sunderland III
172, 304 (Pol), 407 (RCAF), 612 Sqns	Chivenor, Devon	Wellington XIV
524 Sqn	Davidstowe Moor, Cornwall	Wellington XIII
816 (FAA) Sqn	Perranporth, Cornwall	Swordfish II
849 (FAA), 850 (FAA) Sqns	Perranporth, Cornwall	Avenger I
838 (FAA) Sqn	Harrowbeer, Devon	Swordfish

Attached

103 (USN), 105 (USN), 110 (USN), (det) 114 (USN) Sqns		Liberator

Abbreviations:
Cz = Czech
FAA = Fleet Air Arm
Fr = French
Pol = Polish
RAAF = Royal Australian Air Force
RNZAF =Royal New Zealand Air Force
RCAF = Royal Canadian Air Force
ALG = Advance landing ground
Sqn = Squadron

'The RAF on D-Day' by Peter M. Corbell, in the October 1972 issue of *Air Pictorial* gives a detailed list of RAF unit locations on June 6, 1944.

Luftwaffe

Main Headquarters

Headquarters, Luftflotte III	Paris
Jagdkorps II Main fighter defence	Coulommiers
Fliegerkorps II Close-support fighters	Compiègne
Fliegerkorps X Anti-shipping units	Angers
Fliegerkorps IX Long-range bombers	Beauvais
Fliegerdivision II Torpedo bombers	Avignon
Jagddivison 4 Day and night fighters	Metz
Jagddivision 5 Day and night fighters	Coulommiers
Regional Fighter Commands:	
4	St Pol
5	Bernay
Brittany	Rennes
Southern France	Aix

Luftflotte 3
Order of Battle for the beginning of June 1944

Unit (by function)	Aircraft	Strength	Serviceable
Close reconnaissance:			
N.A.Gr.13	Fw190	42	24
	Me109		
Long-range reconnaissance:			
F.A.Gr.5	Ju290:Ju188	15	6
1/(F)33	Ju188:Ju88	7	3
Sonder Aufkl.St.Ob.d.L	Ar240:Ju88	3	0
1/(F)121	Me410	9	3
3/(F)122	Ju188:Ju88	8	2
Gr.Stab.123	Ju188:Fw190	3	3
3/(F)123	Ju88	9	3
4/(F)123	Me109	10	6
5/(F)123	Fw190:Me109	12	8
6/(F)123	Ju188:Ju88	5	0
		81	34
Day fighters:			
Stab JG.2	Fw190:Me109	8	4
I/JG.2	Fw190	19	14
II/JG.2	Me109	13	11
III/JG.2	Fw190	29	19
Stab JG.26	Fw190	2	2
I/JG.26	Fw190	33	23
II/JG.26	Fw190	32	25
III/JG.26	Me109	37	21
Stab ZG.1	Ju88	2	2
I/ZG.1	Ju88	30	25
III/ZG.1	Ju88	23	12
		228	158

Unit (by function)	Aircraft	Strength	Serviceable
Night fighters:			
Stab NJG.4	Ju88	2	0
I/NJG.4	Ju88:Me110	16	7
II/NJG.4	Me110:Do217	20	12
III/NJG.4	Me110:Do217	19	10
I/NJG.5	Me110	15	9
III/NJG.5	Me110	18	8
5 Jagd Div	Me109	2	1
		52	47

Luftflotte 3 operations in Northern France, 1944:-

A 1,000kg (2,205lb) bomb being loaded on to a Ju188, which carried two of these externally, plus sixteen 65kg (143lb) bombs internally

Ju188A with externally carried 1,000kg bombs. Note the bomb aimer's downward vision panel and the 20mm cannon in the nose

A 1,000kg bomb being loaded on to a caterpillar-tracked trolley

The bomb being raised on the trolley for loading under the port wing of the aircraft

A torpedo about to be loaded on to a Ju88 – possibly a Ju88A-17 of Kampfgruppe 28, each aircraft of which carried two 765kg (approx 1685lb) LT F5b torpedoes

Luftflotte 3 bomber aircrew in northern France during early 1944, though the Ju188 (in background) normally carried a four-man crew. Note the inflatable life-jackets and the baggy pockets in the legs of the flying-suits

The Luftwaffe fighter arm in northern France:-

FW190 fighter-bomber in natural camouflage, with two 300-litre (approx 66gal) under-wing tanks

FW190G in close-up, showing overload fuel tanks, its starboard MG 151 machine-gun and a 500kg (just over 1,100lb) bomb on its centreline rack

Like the P-47, the FW190 needed the assistance of a "wing man" in taxying

Loading reconnaissance cameras into an Me109

Ground Attack:
(including dive bombers)

III/SG.4	FW190	40	36

Bombers:

Stab KG.2	Ju188	2	2
I/KG.2	Ju188	12	9
II/KG.2	Ju188	5	0
III/KG.2	Do217	7	1
Stab KG.6	Ju188	1	1
I/KG.6	Ju188	3	2
II/KG.6	Ju88	22	15
1 & 2/KG.66			
(1/KG.66 a special			
pathfinder unit)	Ju188	15	1
III/KG.26	Ju88	35	14
Stab KG.30	Ju88	1	0
I/KG.40 (less 3 St.)	He177	27	12
Stab.K Fl.Korps	Ju88	9	4
II/KG.51	Me410	24	17
Stab KG.54	Ju88	2	0
I/KG.54	Ju88	11	5
III/KG.54	Ju88	14	8
6/KG.76	Ju88:Ju188	16	3
Stab KG.77	Ju88	1	1
I/KG.77	Ju88	28	17
III/KG.77	Ju88	25	8
Stab KG.100	Do217	4	2
III/KG.100	Do217	31	13
I/SKG.	FW190	33	19
		___	___
		328	154
		___	___

Coastal:

2/S.A.Gr 128	Ar196	12	10
1(F) S.A.Gr 129	BV222	4	2
		___	___
		16	12
		___	___

Transport:

IV/TG.4	Leo451	31	13
II/Fl.Korps Trsp. St.	Ju52	13	8
IX/Fl.Korps Trsp. St.	Ju52	9	6
Trsp. Fl. St. Hansa	Leo451	11	4
		___	___
		64	31
		___	___
	Total	891	496
		___	___

Abbreviations:
Gr = Gruppe, i.e. Group/Wing
JG. = Jagdgeschwader, i.e. Fighter Group (literally 'Squadron')
NJG = Nachtjagdgeschwader, i.e. Nightfighter Group
ZG = Zerstoerergeschwader, i.e. Heavy Fighter Group
KG = Kampfgeschwader, i.e. Bomber Group
Stab = Headquarters
N.A. = Close reconnaissance
F.A. = Long-range reconnaissance
S.A. = Maritime reconnaissance
Sonder Auflkl = Special reconnaissance
St. = Staffel, i.e. constituent unit of a 'Gruppe'
Fl Korps = Flieger Korps, i.e. Air Corps
Trsp = Transport

Chapter 3

Aircraft Involved in Overlord

Luftwaffe, RAF and USAAF

Luftwaffe, RAF and USAAF types of aircraft described in the following pages are those which played a significant part in operations over Western Europe during the period covered by this book. Experimental machines, prototypes and aircraft not at that time either under production or in service have not therefore been included.

Arado Ar196
Designed originally to operate in a shipboard reconnaissance role, the **Ar196A-1** two-seat float plane entered service in 1939, equipping many of the German Navy's principal warships. A major variant with improved armament, the **Ar196A-3** went into production a year later for use with land-based units engaged in coastal and sea reconnaissance, patrol and attack missions. Major areas of deployment included the Mediterranean and the Adriatic where they attacked small ships and submarines and protected Axis convoys; and the English Channel where they hampered RAF Coastal Command's anti-U-boat patrols. A third version, the **Ar196A-5,** was also produced.

Arado Ar234 Blitz
When the Allies were establishing their bridgehead in Normandy, this jet bomber/reconnaissance aircraft was being put into production in Germany. Thus, although its prototype had first flown in December 1943, it could not be used operationally during Operation *Overlord* itself; but the fact that this, the world's first operational turbojet bomber, and the Messerchmitt Me262 were both produced by the Germans in 1944 made it all the more urgent that the Allied invasion of Europe should have taken place then and not later, for the Ar234 could soon have proved a serious manned bomber threat to the Allies. Indeed, a four-engined version (with four BMW 003 turbojets mounted in pairs, anticipating the B-52 engine configuration) flew for the first time early in 1944. An additional sinister fact for the Allies was that jet aircraft used low-grade fuel and did not pose supply problems for the Luftwaffe. Its Ar234s were used for reconnaissance **(Ar234B-1)** and as bombers **(Ar234B-2)**, the latter eventually taking part in the final Luftwaffe offensive in the West, against Allied airfields in Belgium, the Netherlands and northern France in January 1945. While the Ar234B, with a bomb load of two tons, had a top speed of 470 mph at 19,700ft, its four-engined successor the **Ar234C** had a top speed of 546mph—indicating what a tough proposition it might have proved for RAF and USAAF fighters to intercept.

An Arado 234B twin-jet bomber or reconnaissance aircraft, which went into service with the Luftwaffe in June 1944

Blohm and Voss Bv222 Wiking

Largest flying-boat to attain operational status in World War II, the type was conceived as a transatlantic passenger carrier, but was converted for military use in 1941, flying transport and maritime reconnaissance missions. Fewer than 20 prototype and production versions were built, of which four were based with 1(F) S.A.Gr.129 at Biscarosse in SW France in June 1944. However, the unit was disbanded after the D-day landings and the aircraft transferred to Norway.

Dornier Do217

This twin-engined, twin-tailed aircraft presented a threefold threat to the Allies in 1944—as a conventional bomber, as a night fighter and as a launcher of unconventional bombs against shipping. In the first of these roles it took part in the final Luftwaffe bombing offensive against Britain, mounted by Fliegerkorps IX from bases in northern France and the Low Countries. This began in January 1944 with attacks on London and ended in April, when Portsmouth and Plymouth were attacked, in an attempt to frustrate Allied invasion preparations. The Do217s which took part in these operations were **K-1s,** which like most of the sub-types of this aircraft had radial engines, BMW 801s; however a similar bomber sub-type, the **M-1,** had DB 603 liquid-cooled engines. This alternative powerplant installation was a safeguard against shortages in production. The Do217 night-fighter role was performed by the **J** sub-type; this had been developed from the basic bomber aircraft (the E version) and carried radar equipment for locating Lancasters and Halifaxes, and heavy forward-firing armament—four 20mm MG FF and four 7.92mm MG 17 guns—for destroying its quarry over the German homeland. The third role performed by Do217s, that of launching unconventional (not free-falling) bombs, was the prerogative of the **E-5** and **K-2** sub-types. The former had carriers under its wings from which were launched Hs293 radio-controlled glider bombs, the earliest operational guided missiles, used against Allied convoys. The K-2 had even more powerful air-to-ground weapons, two Fritz-X 1,400kg radio-controlled armour-piercing bombs, for use against warships. A greater wingspan than the other Do217s enabled the K-2s to climb to 20,000ft to launch their guided bombs. In the final attack of the 1944 Luftwaffe "blitz" against Britain, Fritz-Xs were lauched against warships at Plymouth, though fortunately for the Allies they failed to inflict much damage. Nevertheless in the weeks before D-day these weapons and their carriers were potentially a considerable danger to invasion preparations.

Focke-Wulf FW190

About half the Luftwaffe fighter units which faced the Allies in the west during the early months of 1944 were equipped with this type, the remainder having the Me109; and for both machines the RAF and USAAF pilots who met them in combat had a healthy respect. From the Luftwaffe point of view, the FW190 was more effective in defence against the B-17s and B-24s of the US 8th Air Force on daylight attacks because of its powerful armament—four 20mm MG 151 cannons and two 13mm MG 131 machine-guns. Unfortunately, German fighter production was geared to the Me109, and when the virtues of the FW190 were realised the demand for it could not be adequately supplied. Among these virtues were its effective ailerons, giving it a rate of roll superior to that of the Spitfire, and rapid acceleration in a dive. However, the latter asset could prove a disadvantage if the FW190 were made to dive too steeply from too great an altitude, for compressibility troubles could then occur causing the pilot to lose control. Another limitation in the earlier versions of this fighter was a rapid falling-off in performance above 21,000ft. However, installation of a power boost in the **FW190D-12** gave it the kind of height and speed—37,000ft and 453mph—it needed for attacks from above the American bomber formations, whose escorting Mustangs would be tackled by lower groups of FW190s. Thus in its defensive role the radial-engined Focke-Wulf fighter was the most dangerous opponent the 8th Air Force had to face until the advent of the Me262s. In an offensive role, the fighter bomber version (**FW190G**), carried either a 1,100lb or 2,200lb bomb under the fuselage. Before Operation *Overlord* concentrated the activities of Luftflotte 3 on defence, some of its FW190s were used for hit-and-run attacks against English south coast towns, and at low level the only RAF aircraft which could catch them were the Typhoons. Fortunately for the Allies, a good deal was known about the FW190, as a captured example had been test flown at the Royal Aircraft Establishment during the war and its virtues and weakenesses assessed, for the benefit of fighter pilots operating against it.

Heinkel He177 Greif

First flown in November 1939, a large number of prototype and pre-production versions of this heavy bomber were built, many of which suffered serious powerplant and structural problems. Initial production version was the **He177A-1;** a subsequent version, **He177A-3,** was used briefly to fly emergency supply missions on the Eastern Front in early 1943, although several were lost through engine fires. Final major variant to enter service was the **He177A-5.** From October 1943 He177s were used as Hs293 missile carriers in the anti-convoy and U-boat co-operation missions flown by II./KG 40; this unit being transferred temporarily from Luftflotte 3 to Luftflotte 2 during the Allied landings at Anzio early in 1944. The type was operated by I./KG 40 in the bomber offensive against England in the early months of 1944. During the early phases of the invasion of Normandy the anti-shipping attacks carried out by IX Fliegerkorps were to prove largely ineffective and by mid-July all Luftwaffe anti-shipping units were withdrawn from France except for one He177 unit engaged in meteorological work. He177s were also in service on the Eastern Front during 1944 but, as the German fuel situation deteriorated (aggravated by Spaatz's 'oil plan'), fewer and fewer He177s were able to remain operational.

Junkers Ju88

Of all the forms in which this versatile aircraft appeared during its long life with the Luftwaffe (it first flew in 1936 and operated throughout the war), the Allies had three to worry about in 1944: the **Ju88S,** an improved bomber version with the more powerful engines of the Ju88A; the **Ju88G** night fighter; and the **Ju88H,** a long-range model which could be used for either reconnaissance or fighting duties. When the last German manned bomber attack in force was made against the UK by the Luftwaffe from France in early 1944, the Ju88S provided a main component of the force commanded by Generalmajor D. Peltz. Heavy losses were suffered, chiefly from Mosquito night fighters, though those Ju88S crews who did high-level target-marking (from 30,000ft or above) enjoyed comparative immunity. By contrast, the Luftwaffe's own night-fighter teams using the Ju88G took heavy toll of RAF Bomber Command Halifaxes and Lancasters operating over Germany in the *Pointblank* offensive which preceded Operation *Overlord.* Equipped with an SN-2 search radar, the Ju88Gs would find and join the long bomber streams, generally making their attacks from behind and below the target aircraft. One advantage of the Ju88G over the Me110 as a night fighter was that the former had longer endurance; Me110s were more likely to run out of fuel and have to force-land. Like the Beaufighter and Mosquito night fighters of the RAF, Ju88Gs had two-men crews, pilot and radar operator; success in the night skies over Germany, as over Britain, was very much a team operation. The Ju88H caused the Allies concern during 1944 in two ways: first, because of its reconnaissance capabilities, since any fore-knowledge of the build-up of the invasion fleets had to be denied to the Germans at all costs; secondly, because some of this version were used as the lower half of a fighter-bomber combination known as Mistel (Mistletoe)—the bomber, carrying a 7,700lb warhead, being guided to its target by a Me109 or FW190 control aircraft. This desperate weapon, a potential threat to warships and to D-day shipping, did not bring the Germans much success and the Ju88 hardly deserved such a fate.

Junkers Ju188

Immensely popular with its aircrews, the Ju188 was a development of the Ju88, several versions being delivered for bomber, pathfinder and reconnaissance operations during 1943 and 1944. The type was in service with the units which carried out the strategic bomber offensive against England in early 1944 but had been withdrawn totally from bomber operations before the end of that year. However more than 500 reconnaissance versions remained operational until the end of the war.

Junkers Ju290

A development of the Ju90 transport aircraft, in service from early 1943. Variants within Series A production included **A-1** (transport); **A-2, A-3, A-4** and **A-5** (reconnaissance); **A-6** (transport); **A-7** (bomber/reconnaissance); **A-8** (reconnaissance); **A-9** (ultra long-range reconnaissance). Fifty-five were built. Four subsequent series were proposed but were not produced.

Messerschmitt Me109G

Allowing for its capacity to match the Allies' Spitfires and Thunderbolts, though it could be out-turned and out-dived by the Mustangs, this Luftwaffe fighter was able to strike up a complementary partnership with the FW190, providing a formidable defensive collaboration against RAF and USAAF fighters. One advantage the Me109 had in this tactical situation was that its comparatively short endurance (about 80 minutes' flying) did not prove a disability in operations near to Luftwaffe bases. Acting in a defensive role, it did not have two Channel crossings to make as in 1940 when on the offensive. A disadvantage from which it suffered in 1944, however, was that its pilots were no longer as skilful as they had been in the Battle of Britain. Though the German training programme was producing fighter pilots in numbers, they did not have the requisite skill and experience, and many of them found the Me109G difficult to handle. It was tricky for a beginner when on or near the ground, with its narrow-track undercarriage and its tendency to drop a wing at low speed. On a course of about 30hr flying, the new Luftwaffe fighter pilots just had time to familiarise themselves with basic manoeuvres in the Me109G, leaving little opportunity for combat training before tangling with the Spitfires, P-47s and P-51s. Those who survived long enough against the Allied onslaught, however, had in the Me109G a fine fighting aeroplane. In co-operation with the more heavily armed and armoured FW190s which tackled the 8th Air Force B-17s and B-24s, the 109s engaged the bombers' escorting Thunderbolts and Mustangs. While the Me109, as a type, had been in service since the beginning of the war like its rival the Spitfire it had likewise been greatly developed; and the Me109G version, with 1,800hp Daimler-Benz DB 605D engine, was produced in the largest numbers. Though its Luftwaffe partner the FW190 had a better performance at altitude, the Me109G—in experienced hands—was respected by its opponents throughout the war.

Messerschmitt Me110

It was in the night figher role that this twin-engined two-seater made its most effective contribution to Luftwaffe firepower during the Second World War; and it was in the *Pointblank* offensive prior to Operation *Overlord* that RAF bombers suffered most from Me110 interceptions. For though Luftwaffe night fighter units were gradually being re-equipped with Ju88s, the Me110s still formed the major part of Germany's airborne defences against the Lancasters and Halifaxes. Equipped with radar aids like *SN-2, Naxos-Z* and *Flensburg,* they would find their way into the bomber streams, where their forward- and upward-firing cannons caused heavy losses. Both *Naxos-Z* and *Flensburg* were homing devices, which picked up respectively the bombers' H_2S emissions and tail-warning radar signals, guiding the fighters to their targets. Though the Me110s had both the aids and the armament to seek out and to destroy Bomber Command aircraft, their equipment tended to detract from their performance. Me110s had started the war as day fighters and fighter-bombers, but their weaknesses had been exposed once they came up

Radar array on the nose of a Messerschmitt Me110, which was used effectively by the Luftwaffe as a night-fighter against the aircraft of RAF Bomber Command

Messerschmitt Me262, the first jet fighter to go into service, operated successfully by the Luftwaffe–though in small numbers–in the closing stages of the war

A Messerschmitt Me210 V13 twin-engined fighter-bomber which was not successful, because it was under-powered, and its successor the Messerschmitt Me410 used for attacks on unescorted day bombers

against a determined air defence like that of RAF Fighter Command in the Battle of Britain. During their encounters, the Spitfire and Hurricane pilots found Me110s easy to shoot down, for they were lightly built and not so manoeuvrable as the Me109s, and only succeeded against the RAF fighters if they had the advantage of surprise. In night operations, their radar devices gave them this advantage over the bombers; they did not require manoeuvrability, and their armament—especially the upward-firing cannon—proved lethal against many a Lancaster and Halifax.

Messerschmitt Me262

Although the Me262 had the distinction of being the first turbojet aircraft to enter unit service (in the early summer of 1944), a series of long delays had already robbed the Luftwaffe of a fighter which might well have proved an invaluable weapon against the intensive Allied air activity prior to D-day. Moreover, decisions regarding the deployment and tactical use of the aircraft in 1944-45 irreparably damaged its potential effectiveness in the post D-day phase. Conceived as early as 1938, the first production models **(Me262A-la Schwalbe)** were delivered for trials in May 1944. Some of these aircraft, although not officially in combat service, encountered Allied aircraft during this period. However, at this juncture, Hitler ordered the type be converted to a fighter-bomber. As a result, after further delays, a new version **(Me262A-2a Sturmvogel)** was produced, its two 550lb bombs mounted beneath the nose adversely affecting the aircraft's performance. Reluctant approval was given to continue fighter production alongside that of the fighter-bomber. Several other variants were proposed but not put into production before the war ended.

Messerschmitt Me410

This twin-engined fighter-bomber, developed from the earlier (unsuccessful) Me210, was a German equivalent of the DH Mosquito. Though it looked like the Me210 it had more powerful engines, giving it greater speed and a higher ceiling; it could achieve 390 mph and operate at over 32,000ft, attributes which made it suitable for operations over Britain during late 1943 and early 1944, on intruder or reconnaissance missions. It could carry over 4,000lb of bombs and was used in small numbers during the last Luftwaffe bomber offensive in early 1944 against London and other cities in the British Isles. Its main function, however, came to be that of a destroyer of Allied bombers over Germany. For this purpose it had heavy forward-firing armament—normally four 20mm cannon and four machine-guns in the nose, four wing-mounted 210mm rocket launchers and two remotely controlled rearward-firing machine-guns; but some Me410s went into action with a 50mm cannon projecting from the nose. The principle of the latter was that of the naval broadside or tank cannon in practice; but the BK 5 cannon used had a low rate of fire and suffered from frequent stoppages. Like this weapon, which was fitted to it in a desperate attempt to counter the *Pointblank* offensive, the Me410 itself was not popular. Its speed and manoeuvrability were gained at the expense of safety; at least one version had a 60lb/sq ft wing loading, and this led to high approach and landing speeds, which could make handling difficult under adverse conditions or at night. Engine failure increased this difficulty, and pilots were advised not to attempt an overshoot. Additionally, the Me410 suffered from undercarriage unserviceabilities, which probably stemmed from the complexity of its retraction system.

Airspeed Horsa
This glider, towed by an Albermarle, Dakota or Halifax, was the transport for all the British troops who went into battle by that means during the early hours of D-day on June 6, 1944. Each Horsa could carry 30 armed soliders, plus extra weapons like Bren guns, mortars and bombs. With two pilots, the total load was about 8,000lb, rather more than the glider itself weighed; all-up weight was approximately 15,500lb. As it had a tricycle undercarriage (the main wheels of which could be jettisoned after take-off) the Horsa sat on the runway in a flying attitude behind its tug. This probably helped it to get airborne quickly, but the glider pilots needed to exercise care in maintaining a correct attitude behind the tug aircraft. Once the Horsas reached their release point, their independent flying time was brief, for with an 8,000lb load and at an airspeed of about 90 mph they lost 800ft of height every minute. This meant that if they were released at, say, 2,400ft they were on the ground in three minutes. During that brief prelude to action, in a sudden silence which must have been eerie and ominous to the 30 men sitting in the rear of the fuselage, the Horsa pilots had to control the rate of descent through the night skies over Normandy, to look out for obstructions and to identify their landing area from pre-flight briefings. When the glider jarred and skidded along the ground, either on its main wheels or on a sprung skid, its direction could be controlled by the castoring nosewheel (unless this had been broken off on impact). The fuselage to the rear of the wings was hinged, and this enabled the troops to get out quickly once the Horsa had come to rest. Used in the Sicilian landings in 1943, these Airspeed gliders again proved their worth on D-day, their most brilliant single application being in the capture of a swing bridge over the Caen canal—one Horsa touching down less than 50 yards from its occupants' objective.

Armstrong Whitworth AW41 Albermarle
Four squadrons equipped with this type of aircraft towed Horsa gliders to Normandy in the early hours of D-day, June 6, 1944, and a flight of one of the squadrons (No 295) acted as pathfinders for the 6th Airborne Division parachute drop near Caen. Thus in Operation *Overlord,* as during the previous year in the airborne assault on Sicily, the Albermarle gained the military fame which had been denied to it in the bomber role for which it was originally intended. This change of employment was not due to any intrinsic fault (the Albermarle had "no virtues and no vices", according to one test pilot) but to obsolescence; for by the time it was ready for service the four-engined bombers were on the scene. Its other distinction, apart from honourable employment with the airborne forces, was that of being the first British aircraft with a nose-wheel undercarriage to be built in quantity for the RAF.

Auster IV
Light aircraft in service with squadrons of No 83 and 84 Groups of the Allied Expeditionary Air Force as Air Observation Posts, operating from limited, unprepared air strips.

Avro Lancaster
Some 43 squadrons in RAF Bomber Command were operating Lancasters at the time of the *Pointblank* bomber offensive which preceded Operation *Overlord,* and they were a

Mosquito XVI, which had a pressurised cabin and could carry a 4,000lb bomb, of No 571 Sqn of the Pathfinder Force

This type of Mosquito, a Mark XVIII belonging to No 248 Sqn and wearing its D-day indentification markings, carried an armament of four 0.313in machine-guns and a six-pounder cannon – protruding below the aircraft's nose – and was used for operations against returning U-boats and enemy surface shipping, in the Bay of Biscay and Norwegian fiords

mighty weapon in Allied hands. Their bomb load, only the Lancaster could carry the 22,000lb *Grand Slam* bomb, their speed, their use of radar aids, their docile handling qualities and the strength and simplicity of their design made them ideal for production in quantity and deployment in large numbers. Had it not been for the urgent demands of the growing bomber offensive, the four-engined Lancaster might never have been developed from the twin-engined Manchester which the RAF Air Staff originally specified, though the basic design was not substantially modified. It was wedding the well-proved Rolls-Royce Merlin engine to an Avro airframe which created the Lancaster; and it was the skill and courage of RAF aircrew, going out night after night over Europe in response to the operational instructions of Bomber Command headquarters, which created the Lancaster legends. Operations immediately before D-day were of a different calibre from those which Lancaster squadrons normally undertook in their offensive against German industrial resources. Yet, so far as the aircraft was concerned, the change of role to tactical support was one taken in its stride; for it was versatile in bombing roles, and its crews had great confidence in the Lancaster's abilities. Defensively, it was vulnerable from below, and this weakness was exploited by the Luftwaffe night fighters; it suffered also from weight of numbers, in that once the German defences had established the target heading of a bomber stream, they could locate and destroy its components. In such circumstances, even the Lancaster's speed could not save it; but given the odds stacked against a night bomber in 1942-45, the Lancaster crews had as good a chance as any save those of the Mosquito.

de Havilland Mosquito

No part of the RAF, in its Order of Battle prior to the Normandy landings, was without the DH98 Mosquito in one form or another; it was probably the most versatile aircraft produced by any country during the Second World War. Originally, however, the concept of an unarmed bomber with a two-man crew did not appeal to the RAF. When thinking ran on the lines of a large crew and heavy self-defensive armament, the idea of a little wooden aeroplane, relying on speed for immunity from interception, was unacceptable. However, once the Mosquito had been produced and put into service, its acceptability knew no bounds; and the parts it played in operations prior to *Overlord* showed how wide were its capabilities. In Bomber Command its logistics were probably more impressive than those of any other type: it needed far fewer crew members and its engine maintenance was arithmetically half that of the Lancasters and Halifaxes; yet it could mark targets for the bomber stream or take a 4,000lb bomb to Berlin. In the 2nd Tactical Air Force it operated in the light bomber and fighter-bomber roles, or as a night fighter, or on photographic reconnaissance. In Coastal Command it made anti-shipping strikes; and it played a dominant role in the activities of No 100 Group, whose night intruder and radar countermeasures operations caused confusion among the German defences. The Mosquito not only satisfied those who planned the offensives which led up to the Normandy landings, for its losses were comparatively light and its effectiveness correspondingly great, whether using bombs, rockets, cannon-shells or cameras; it also satisfied those concerned with the political direction of the war on the Allied side, for it gained spectacular successes like breaching the walls of Amiens prison to release the Gestapo's captives. Significantly too, the Mosquito set a precedent for the post-war RAF jet bombers, flying fast and high and possessing no self-defensive armament.

General Aircraft Hamilcar

This was a big aircraft, easily the largest of the three types of glider used by the Allies for their landings in Normandy during the early hours of D-day. It had a wingspan of 110ft—as great as that of a B-24 Liberator—and in length (68ft) was nearly a foot longer. With a load of eight tons (either military vehicles or heavy equipment), and because of its size, it needed a four-engined tow. This was usually provided by a Halifax or a Stirling. Since the maximum speed at which a Hamilcar could be towed was 150mph and its stalling speed was 65mph, the Army pilot did not have much flexibility of decision once he had been cast off; and since the June 6th landings were made in darkness, when obstructions on the ground could not be identified until it was probably too late to avoid them, the success of Hamilcars in taking critical equipment into battle was remarkable. Made entirely of wood, they had vehicle rails along the fuselage floor, which could be adjusted to suit the load carried—whether tank, Bren carriers, scout cars or mobile Bofors gun. In the sides of the fuselage were exhaust extractors, so that engines could be started up before the Hamilcar touched down, and vehicles driven out through the hinged door and into battle as soon as the big glider was on the ground.

Handley Page Halifax

Partner with the Avro Lancaster in the RAF night bomber offensive against Germany, the Halifax played its part in *Pointblank* operations preceding D-day. Like the Lancaster, it had originated in a twin-engined specification, but unlike that type it had no twin-engined predecessor in Bomber Command. While it was used in less spectacular ways than the Lancaster, it was employed more widely; for example, in No 100 Group on counter-measure operations, in Coastal Command on long-range maritime reconnaissance, and as a glider tug taking the big Hamilcar gliders with their eight-ton loads into the Normandy battle area. While the more familiar profile of the Lancaster is that with inline (Rolls-Royce Merlin) engines, the correspondingly more familiar Halifax profile is that with radial (Bristol Hercules) engines, though different marks of both types had alternative powerplants. In the period prior to D-day, some 23 squadrons of the Bomber Command main force were equipped with the Halifax, and the type played a notable part in supporting the French Maquis, who were engaged in harassing the Germans before the Normandy landings; it was used also by one of the special duty squadrons which undertook clandestine missions for the Resistance movement operating in France before the Allied liberation.

Hawker Typhoon

Before and after D-day this fighter played an impressive part in supporting the Allied landings and subsequent advance across Europe. Squadrons of the 2nd Tactical Air Force equipped with it attacked radar installations, gun sites, troop concentrations, convoys, trains and tanks. Its armament was formidable: with eight rockets (each with a 60lb HE or 25lb armour-piercing head) in addition to its four 20mm cannon, its firepower was comparable to that of a broadside from a cruiser and could penetrate the most heavily armoured tanks. Alternatively, two 1,000lb bombs were carried on under-wing racks. Thus the Typhoon was probably the most effective ground-attack aircraft of the Second World War, though it was originally designed as an intercepter, and troubles which occurred after its introduction into service in 1942 almost caused RAF Fighter

Teeth for a Typhoon: fitting the last of four rockets into the rails under the starboard wing. Above them, two of the aircraft's four 20mm cannon

Command to withdraw it. These troubles sprang mainly from its very powerful (2,200 hp) Napier Sabre 24-cylinder inline liquid-cooled sleeve-valve engine, and were of two kinds: either jamming of the sleeves, causing a cylinder to blow up; or vibration from the engine coinciding with vibration in the tail, inducing structural failure, which could also occur when a violent yaw followed sudden deceleration. Had the Typoon been given a longer development period its initial weaknesses would have been eradicated, but the Air Ministry was anxious to get it into service to counter the FW190 tip-and-run raiders across the Channel, and its speed at low level made it successful in this. By D-day the Typhoon's early troubles had been overcome; it was a well-proved machine, equipping 20 squadrons, and in the ground-support role proved a devastating asset for the Allies in their hard-won progress to the Rhine and beyond.

Short Stirling

By the time of the *Pointblank* combined bomber offensive and of Operation *Overlord*, Stirlings had been almost completely withdrawn from Bomber Command squadrons (only three of which were still operating them, plus one special duty squadron), but were in use with No 38 Group for towing Horsa gliders. Four squadrons of **Mk IVs,** carrying less armament than the Mk Is and IIIs, and modified internally, performed the latter task. In view of this demotion to a passive role, it was ironic that the Stirling had been the original RAF four-engined bomber, specified by the Air Ministry in 1936 and brought into service in 1940; its successors, the Avro Lancaster and Handley Page Halifax, were both developments of twin-engined specifications. While the latter types at different times had both inline and radial engines (Merlin or Hercules) the Stirling was consistently powered by radial engines, principally the Bristol Hercules XI (Mk I) and XVI (Mk III), although the small number of Mk IIs built had Wright Cyclones. Its withdrawal from bomber operations was due to its increasing vulnerability to German defences at the lower altitudes at which it had to fly because of an inadequate service ceiling. This limitation derived from insufficient wing area, for with a length of 87ft 3in the Stirling had a wing span of 99ft 1in, while comparable measurements for the Lancaster and Halifax respectively were 69ft 6in/102ft and 70ft 1in/104ft 2in. Another of the Stirling's liabilities was its shoulder-wing configuration which meant that the undercarriage legs were long and the aircraft angle relative to the ground was steep, adding an extra hazard on landing. Nevertheless, Stirlings made an impressive addition to Bomber Command offensive capability before the Halifax and Lancaster appeared, being strongly built and able to absorb a great deal of punishment.

Supermarine Spitfire

Almost without exception, the Spitfire fighter squadrons in the 2nd Tactical Air Force during the months preceding D-day had **Mk IXs** and the reconnaissance squadrons **Mk XIs.** With the Mk IX version, powered by a Rolls-Royce Merlin 61, 63, 63A, 66 or 70 engine of over 1,650hp, the Spitfire regained the superiority over the FW190 which it had lost with the Mk V version; the **PR.XI** was similarly powered. As the war moved into Europe, however, the fact that the Spitfire had been designed as a defensive fighter—a role it had performed brilliantly in the Battle of Britain—became evident in its lack of range. With a radius of action of about 175 miles, its effectiveness as an escort fighter for daylight bombers was limited. It could never operate over Germany from the UK, as the Mustang could, and it was the latter type which made a crucial contribution to Allied air superiority by going all the way with the USAAF Fortresses and Liberators. The contribution the Spitfire made to RAF fighting capability and morale throughout the Second World War, however, was an enormous one; and to the Luftwaffe its name became synonymous with 'fighter'. The quality of its original design by R. J. Mitchell was such that, although over a decade its power and armament were doubled, the original shape of the aeroplane was never substantially altered.

Boeing B-17 Flying Fortress

The 'Flying Fortress', so called because it carried more self-defensive armament than any other bomber in the Second World War, became almost a symbol of the massive American contribution to the European air offensive. Yet when initially operated by the RAF in 1941 it was not successful, partly because the version used (B-17C) did not possess the protective firepower of the -E, -F, and -G models, and partly because Bomber Command had by then turned to night operations. Sceptical about daylight bombing because of high losses early in the war, Bomber Command operated the B-17s at too high an altitude for their best performance, and did not have enough of them for employment in numbers which would have made their concentrated firepower effective. The US Army Air Force, however, stuck to its policy of daylight bombing for which the B-17 (and B-24) had been designed; and by 1944, with the 8th Air Force hammering at

Germany from bases in the UK and the 15th AF mounting an offensive against German and satellite-country targets from Italy, the policy had been vindicated. With the support of long-range P-51s and P-47s, the B-17s and B-24s made the CBO (combined bomber offensive) effective by adding daylight attacks on the German heartland to those of RAF Bomber Command by night. In this high-altitude warfare the B-17 was an ideal weapon, strongly built, docile to fly and able to give a good account of itself against German fighters with its thirteen heavy-calibre (0.50in) machine-guns. It had extensive armour plating and self-sealing fuel tanks, and with the Norden bomb-sight its crews were able to achieve remarkably accurate results on targets 20,000ft below.

Consolidated B-24 Liberator

In the RAF-USAAF combined bomber offensive which in early 1944 paved the way for the Allied landings in Normandy, B-24s played their part side by side with the B-17s and in many respects were similar: a ten-man crew, heavy self-defensive armament (ten 0.50in machine-guns in the B-24, thirteen in the B-17), Norden bomb-sights for precison high-altitude attacks and four radial engines of 1,200 hp (Pratt & Whitney Twin Wasps in the B-24, Wright Cyclones in the B-17). But the B-24 had a longer range and smaller bomb load than the B-17: a range of over 2,000 miles as against 1,850 and a maximum load of 12,800lb compared with 17,600lb. A unique feature of the B-24 amongst Allied heavy bombers was its tricycle undercarriage, and its long (110ft) high-aspect ratio wing which extended at shoulder level from a deep fuselage. The B-24 would obtain its best cruising speed if climbed above, then dived down to, the intended altitude. Like the B-17, it had impressive powers of self-preservation in hostile skies, and it was produced in even greater numbers than its famous contemporary: more than 18,000 B-24s were built (at the peak of their wartime production, Ford in Detroit were turning out one every 24 hours) compared with nearly 13,000 B-17s. The 8th Air Force in the UK at the time of D-day was using B-24s for both bombing and reconnaissance duties.

Douglas A-20 Havoc/Boston

Like its famous contemporary in the light bomber role, the North American B-25, the A-20 had a tricycle undercarriage configuration; it was easy to land and stable to fly, being particularly well behaved under asymmetric conditions. In the months before D-day these tough machines, with their reliable 1,600 hp Wright Double Cyclone radial engines, were used by both the RAF 2nd Tactical Air Force and the USAAF 9th Air Force in daylight bombing attacks and on intruder missions against enemy airfields. According to its duty, the A-20 (known also as **P-70** in a night-fighter version) could carry up to 4,000lb of bombs—2,000lb in its weapon bay and 2,000lb externally—or was armed alternatively with nine 0.50in machine guns/four 0.50in machine guns plus four 20mm cannon. Its narrow but deep fuselage accommodated a crew of three—pilot, navigator/bomb aimer (in the nose) and wireless operator.

Douglas C-47 Skytrain/C-53 Skytrooper/Dakota

This twin-engined (1,200hp Pratt & Whitney Twin Wasps) transport did all the glider-towing and paratroop dropping for the American airborne forces on D-day, 1944, and much of that for the British and Allied soldiers of the Parachute and Glider Pilot Regiments. The C-47/Dakota (known by the latter name in the RAF, which received more than 1,200 under Lend-Lease) was unarmed[1], but went in under fire not only over Normandy but at Arnhem and when the Rhine was crossed by the Allies. It was thus an integral part of the airborne forces' equipment, apart from its employment on all kinds of transport duty in every theatre of the Second World War. Its amenable flying qualities (with a 64ft 5½in fuselage it had a generous wing span of 95ft) endeared it to pilots, and its strong construction enabled it not only to ride out rough conditions with equanimity but to withstand hard usage internally from military personnel and freight. Although the C-47/Dakota first flew as a civil airliner (DC-3) in 1935, and from 1939 to 1945 provided the backbone of American and British military air transport services, it was still in use with commercial airlines in the 1970s.

Lockheed P-38 Lightning

When the Allied ships ploughed their way across the English Channel on D-day, they were given fighter protection by P-38 Lightnings of the USAAF 9th Air Force. This was because these twin-tailed aircraft, with slender booms extending from their two engines and a short fuselage in between, could not be mistaken for anything else by naval gunners. But such deliberate employment of a distinctively shaped machine did not imply that the Lightning's uses were limited to such special occasions; in fact it contributed impressively to five aspects of the European air war, with both the 8th and the 9th US Air Forces. First, it escorted B-17s and B-24s on their daylight missions, though as the sorties got longer this protective role was taken over by the P-51 Mustangs. Secondly, it operated in the 9th AF IX Tactical Air Command as an interceptor, groups in the command's three fighter wings being equipped with Lightnings and Thunderbolts. Thirdly, it was a fighter-bomber, and bombing missions by Lightnings carrying 3,200lb of bombs and flying in formation were often led by an unarmed **P-38J.** This was a conversion to a two-seater configuration with a Perspex nose: it carried a bombardier who used a Norden bomb-sight, the P-38J (or P-38L) acting as target marker for the other Lightnings. Fourthly, in their **F-5** version the P-38s did photographic reconnaissance for both the 8th and 9th Air Forces. The F-5 was a development of the **F-4,** an unarmed PR Lightning with four cameras; the F-5 carried three, four or five cameras according to requirements. Fifthly, in its last manifestation during the European war, the Lightning **P-38L** had 14 rocket launchers, in two batteries of seven, one under each wing. Its normal armament was one 20mm cannon and four 0.50in machine-guns. Throughout its service career, from 1941 onwards, the P-38 Lightning was powered by increasingly larger versions of the Allison V-1710 inline engines—51/55s of 1,325hp in the **P-38G,** 89/91s of 1,425hp in the **-H** and **-J,** and -111/113s of 1,475hp in the **L** version.

Martin B-26 Marauder

This medium bomber was operated with conspicuous success in 1944 by four USAAF groups of 98 Bombardment Wing in IX Bomber Command of the 9th Air Force; yet at least twice in its career it had almost been withdrawn from service. This was because the virtues in its conception, notably speed and defensive armament, created aerodynamic penalties. The weight of the beautifully rounded cigar-shaped fuselage and two Pratt &

---

[1]Paratroop pathfinder aircraft operating in the early hours of D-day were equipped to carry bombs. These bombs were released on crossing the coast to deceive the enemy about the true role of the aircraft.

Whitney 2,000hp Double Wasp engines was carried below a comparatively small wing area, to give maximum performance; but the resultant high wing loading meant that take-off and landing speeds were high, and the handling difficulties experienced initially led to many accidents when crews trained on the B-26 with full fuel and bomb loads. That was in 1941, however, and operational experience with the type had led to a number of improvements being introduced. These resulted in the **B-26B** version, with which the 98 Bombardment Wing groups were equipped (though the -Bs included variants; for example, wing span of the **B-26B-10-MA** was increased from 65ft to 71ft). Yet even in 1943 the operational value of the type had been questioned, for a second time, when Marauders in the 8th Air Force suffered heavy losses on low-level operations against Continental targets from UK bases. In the European theatre, it was not until they had been transferred to the 9th Air Force in November 1943 that they began to come into their own as tactical bombers in support of the forthcoming invasion, particularly on night sorties. In daylight raids, their eleven 0.50in machine-guns gave them formidable defensive firepower when in formation. The RAF had evaluated the Marauder in 1942, was supplied with the type under Lend-Lease and equipped five squadrons in the Middle East; these operated effectively in the Desert Air Force. Like its US contemporaries in the bomber field the B-26 had a tricycle undercarriage, though its Martin contemporary the A-30 Baltimore, designed to RAF requirements, had a tail-wheel configuration. The B-26 had first flown on November 25, 1940, and an initial order was placed for 1,100.

North American B-25 Mitchell
This medium bomber played an equivalent role in the 2nd Tactical Air Force to that of the Martin B-26 Marauder in the USAAF 9th Air Force, and the RAF considered the Mitchell to be an excellent machine. In 2nd TAF the practice was to employ it in sub-formations of five aircraft on daylight operations; in this way its tremendous fire power—thirteen 0.50in machine-guns—would give formidable defensive cover. Another practice in No 2 Group (which had all the UK-based RAF Mitchell squadrons) was to use Mitchells and Mosquitos together in night operations, the former acting as target illuminators for the Mosquito bombers. The B-25 had come into RAF service in 1943, so that by the time of the intensive tactical bombing operations in the first half of 1944 prior to the Allied landings on D-day it was a well-tried weapon, which No 2 Group wielded with devastating results. Its bomb load was 4,000lb; it cruised at 200mph or faster when required (up to 275mph); and these capabilities, coupled with its defensive fire power, its reliable 1,850hp Wright Cyclone radial engines and its good handling qualities, made it well liked by aircrew. Earlier in the war, before its contribution to the European air offensive, the B-25 had had the best advertisement of any bomber for take-off performance. This was when sixteen B-25Bs (versions supplied to the RAF were mainly **-Cs, -Ds** and **-Js,** although it had a small number of **-Bs**) took off from the flight deck of the aircraft carrier USS *Hornet* to attack targets in Japan. Though the results of this spectacular raid were more psychological than physical, it had a morale-boosting effect upon the US pride. Its leader was Lt-Col James H. Doolittle, who at the time of Operation *Overlord* commanded the USAAF 8th Air Force in the UK as Maj-Gen Doolittle. The B-25

itself was named after another famous American air general, William Mitchell, who as a colonel in the 1920s was an outspoken advocate of air power.

North American P-51 Mustang

This Anglo-American fighter came to full operational maturity just when it was most needed, in the early months of 1944 when the Allies were preparing to carry the war into Europe. Its great contribution to the final stage of operations in the west was establishment of air supremacy over Germany by day; in escorting US 8th Air Force bombers to Berlin it made the round-the-clock strategic offensive a practical reality. Yet its origin had not been promising; built to a British specification, it had a limited performance with an Allison powerplant, but when re-engined with a Rolls-Royce Merlin (first a-61, then a-68 built by Packard Motors in the United States) became a real war bird, especially when some operational advantages—like fittings for disposable long-range fuel tanks—were added to the initial fine design. Thus powered and equipped, it went into service with the 8th Air Force in December 1943 and as escort for the B-17s and B-24s made its presence felt with the Luftwaffe fighter defences. It is this role which gave the P-51 its fame in the Second World War, a role which it took over from the P-47 Thunderbolt because of its greater manoeuvrability in combats with Me109s and FW190s. The Merlin-powered versions were the **P-51B** and **C (Mustang III** in the RAF) and **P-51D** (RAF **Mustang IV**), which had a bubble-type cockpit canopy giving better all-round visibility. The P-51D, nearly 8,000 of which were built, also had six 0.50in machine-guns compared with four in the earlier types. The Mustang was also used by the US 9th Air Force for both combat and PR (including low-level photography of the landing beaches before D-day) duties, and by RAF, RCAF and Polish Air Force squadrons, both in the 2nd Tactical Air Force and Air Defence of Great Britain. Product of a unique wartime marriage of British airframe and aero-engine design with American engineering response and productive capacity, the P-51 Mustang came into the Allied ranks just at the time when it could make significant contributions to the *Pointblank* combined bomber offensive and to Operation *Overlord*.

Republic P-47 Thunderbolt

Both the 8th and 9th Air Forces of the USAAF employed this fighter in considerable numbers for the offensive operations leading up to D-day. In the 8th, the strategic bombing force which unlike RAF Bomber Command had its own fighter arm (VIII Fighter Command), the Thunderbolts shared escort duties with the P-38 Lightnings and P-51 Mustangs; in the 9th, Thunderbolts operated in the tactical fighter role (again with Lightnings and Mustangs) in the IXth and XIXth Tactical Air Commands. Thus the P-47 was as versatile as its contemporaries, but what marked it out from them was its size; it was easily the biggest single-engined fighter of the Second World War. Radial-engined like the FW190, it weighed more when empty (10,700lb) than the German fighter did when loaded (9,750lb), and the P-47's loaded weight (17,500lb) was almost three times that of a Spitfire VB's (6,650lb). But the Thunderbolt's heavyweight character did not prevent it being highly successful over Europe in the hands of USAAF fighter pilots. With a powerful engine (Pratt & Whitney Double Wasp, of 2,535hp in the **P-47D,** the most numerous version) and armament of six or eight 0.50in machine-guns, it was a

P-38s returning to their Italian base after escorting 15th AF bombers over Austria

P-51s of the 31st Fighter Group, with red noses and red tail stripes

match for the Luftwaffe FW190s or Me109Gs above 20,000ft, and could catch any of its opponents in a dive. At lower altitudes it was not so successful, until a water-injection system was introduced which boosted its horse-power and increased its speed to well over 400mph. Another disadvantage was that if it was drawn into combat early in its bomber escort duties by the FW190s, and had to fight and shed its under-wing fuel drop tanks, it could not cover the B-17s and B-24s over German territory because its internal fuel range was insufficient. However, when the long-range escort role was taken over by the Mustangs from the end of 1943 the P-47s continued to play an impressive part in establishing Allied daylight air supremacy over Europe in preparation for the Allied invasion, both as intercepter and ground-attack fighters. Strongly built, able to absorb punishment and still get home, they were liked by pilots who flew them and earned the affectionate nickname 'Jug' (short for 'Juggernaut').[1]

Waco CG-4A Hadrian

This was the type of glider which, towed across the Channel by C-47s/53s of the USAAF IXth Troop Carrier Command, landed American airborne troops and their equipment on the dark Normandy fields in the early hours of D-day. About 100 Wacos were employed in this initial assault; they each carried 15 fully equipped soldiers, or a jeep, or a six-pounder gun. Loading was done through the nose, which hinged upwards, and the fuselage had a square configuration. Wacos (called Hadrians by the British) had previously been used in the Sicily landings of 1943, some 240 pilots of the Glider Pilot Regiment converting to them for this operation, having assembled them before getting airborne. One of the RAF pilots who had towed an Airspeed Horsa (the Waco's British equivalent) out from the UK reported that the American glider had four disadvantages: since it was fitted with spoilers instead of flaps, there was some difficulty in losing height and speed for landing; a safety limitation to 125mph on towing speed might make it unsuitable to use with an Albermarle as tug aircraft; because its load was a gun or a jeep, but not both, there was the risk of an immobile weapon or unarmed vehicle unless two Hadrians landed together; and in the event of a heavy landing, the six-pounder was likely to go through the bottom of the glider. These disadvantages, however, seem to have been overcome and Wacos played their part valiantly in the Allied landings. CG-4As were originally manufactured by the Waco Aircraft Co of Troy, Ohio, oldest producers of civil aircraft in the USA (established in 1921); but eventually 16 companies were involved, building nearly 14,000 from 1942 to the end of the war.

---

[1] For a vivid account of P-47 operations during *Overlord*, see *Fighter Pilot: The First American Ace of World War II*, by William R. Dunn (The University Press of Kentucky, 1982).

Chapter 4

The Air Commanders:
American, British and German

American Air Commanders

Lieutenant-General Lewis H. Brereton Commander of the Ninth Air Force, the American element of the Allied Expeditionary Air Force.

Although a graduate of the US Naval Academy Lewis H. Brereton had pursued an Army career and had become an aviator in 1913. During the First World War he served in the Army Air Service in France under Brigadier-General 'Billy' Mitchell, the enterprising and far-sighted commander who, in an attempt to break the deadlock of trench warfare, had proposed dropping a force from the 1st US Division behind German lines, to attack Metz from the rear. Detailed planning for the operation had been assigned to Brereton, and although the operation never materialised, the basic concept provided valuable experience for him and also a foretaste of a task he was to undertake many years later.

By the autumn of 1941 the threat of Japanese aggression was rapidly increasing. The Philippines appeared to be in the most immediate danger and the Americans therefore decided to strengthen the Army Air Force there. Brereton was appointed Commander of the US Far East Air Force under General MacArthur. His initial task was to prepare his command for attack but he was faced with many problems. Describing the state of preparations for war in Manila in 1941, he wrote: " . . . There was a comprehensive project on paper for the construction of additional airfields, but unfortunately little money had been provided prior to my arrival . . .". He found communications to be inefficient and unreliable; there were two untried radar installations; a lack of essential stores and supplies; and uncamouflaged B-17s, visible for 25 miles. Efforts to remedy the situation proved inadequate against the inevitable Japanese assault and his reduced force was limited to the role of reconnaissance until the US surrender in May 1942.

The British were also encountering setbacks, with serious reversals in North Africa. Urgent appeals to the United States resulted in offers of equipment, especially tanks and guns. However, the Americans decided that instead of simply supplying aircraft to reinforce the RAF squadrons they would establish units of their own. Brereton was by this time commanding the Tenth Air Force in India, but on June 23, 1942, he received copies of an order stating: ". . . Brereton will come at once to Middle East with available heavy bombers, with mission to assist Auchinleck. Instruct Brereton all our units in Middle East will come under his command. . . ." Accordingly, on June 28 he took command of the newly formed United States Army Middle East Air Force (USAMEAF).

He immediately initiated a series of co-ordinated strikes against enemy supply lines, with concentrated attacks on Benghazi, Tobruk and on convoys assembling in Greece and Crete and at sea. With the arrival of US fighter units in the theatre from the end of July, he had the inexperienced American pilots integrated into RAF squadrons to be 'blooded', i.e. acclimatised to operational conditions peculiar to the desert.

Fortunately, like the RAF leaders Tedder and Coningham, Brereton was an apostle of the creed of co-operation; thus, when the US Desert Air Task Force came into being on October 22, 1942, prior to the El Alamein offensive, he took personal command, setting up a small staff at the British Advanced Headquarters in the Western Desert both for the sake of gaining experience and of representing US interests.

On November 12, 1942, the USAMEAF became the Ninth Air Force, and the role it played in the following months helped to end the North African campaign, and contributed to Operation *Husky* (the landings in Sicily) and the invasion of Italy. Attacks on Axis supply lines deprived the enemy of much-needed reinforcements and this action was supplemented by raids against strategic targets in southern Europe, the most notable being the Rumanian oil refineries at Ploesti.

This mission was undertaken under Brereton's direction at the height of the Sicilian campaign. Its aim was to destroy a number of key installations in the nine principal refineries. The general layout of the target area was known, and in the period of intensive training and briefing which preceded the raid Brereton made use of a 'dummy' Ploesti to familiarise his crews with their targets. The resultant low-level attack, on August 1, 1943, displayed the immense courage of Brereton's crews, but its success was limited by a series of errors in navigation caused by the loss of the leading aircraft early in the mission. However, the Germans were forced to bring reserve production capacity into use, thereby increasing their vulnerability, while much-needed fuel was lost.

During the North African and Mediterranean campaigns Brereton was to familiarise himself with the principles of tactical ground-air co-ordination. Participating fully in inter-Service, inter-Allied planning, he not only appreciated the necessity for co-operation but was also prepared to accept the proven methods of his fellow commanders, adapting them to the requirements of his own air force. Thus, he created a mobile organisation on the lines of the RAF, adapting the latter's techniques of streamlining and 'leap-frogging' to ensure the greatest possible utilisation of his units.

Accordingly, when Brereton came to the UK in the autumn of 1943 he was experienced in a wide range of air operations. His task was to mould the newly reactivated Ninth Air Force into a tactical command, able to provide direct support to the *Overlord* operations. Many of his colleagues were familiar faces from the Mediterranean, including his British opposite number, Air Marshal Sir Arthur Coningham. Equally familiar were the underlying precepts of the accepted air plans, with integration of British and US capability.

The part played by Brereton's Ninth Air Force in the great offensive prior to June 6, 1944, is related elsewhere. The spirit of co-operation and commitment, coupled with operational prowess, which were the foundations of this effort, owed much to the qualities of the commander.

With the invasion due to begin, Brereton moved to Coningham's Advanced Headquarters at Uxbridge and from there directed his aircraft in their many tasks on D-day itself.

Lieutenant-General Lewis H. Brereton (right) with Air Marshal Sir Arthur Coningham during the former's visit to a 2nd Tactical Air Force station. A B-25 Mitchell is in the background

However, once the Allied foothold had been established on the Continent, Brereton became involved in a change of organisational structure. The existing set-up for airborne operations was a complex and cumbersome arrangement involving the army and the air forces. Even before D-day, proposals had been made for a combined British/US Headquarters Airborne Troops. In approving such an organisation, the Supreme Commander had stated that the commander would need to possess real ability, leadership and experience; furthermore he would have to be an air officer.[1] Brereton was seen to possess these qualities, having already directed the IX Troop Carrier Command as an integral part of the Ninth Air Force. It will also be remembered, coincidentally, that he had been responsible for drawing up those unused plans for airborne operations in the First World War.

Consequently, on August 16, 1944—although taking "a dim view" of the assignment—he became the first Commander of the First Allied Airborne Army. This appointment was to have its frustrations, particularly as he was unable to exploit fully what he considered to be the strategic potential of his force. His Command was, nevertheless, able to contribute usefully to the overall decisive action which was to lead ultimately to Allied victory.

Lieutenant-General James H. Doolittle Commander of the US Eighth Air Force. By the time he became involved in Operation *Overlord,* the career of Major-General James H. Doolittle had included not only outstanding personal achievement but also a considerable contribution to the American war effort.

He began his military aviation career in 1917 in the Army Air Service. In 1922 he made the first flight across the continent of North America in less than twenty-four hours; then, in a period of highly successful air racing, won such coveted trophies as the Schneider in 1925 and the Thompson in 1932. As an experimental engineer in the Air Corps Materiel Division he took a leading part in the development of aircraft blind flying and made the first successful flight on instruments. In recognition of this work he was awarded the Harmon Trophy in 1930. That same year he left the Air Corps to follow a civilian career as aviation specialist with an oil company.

During the 1930s, views like those expressed by the Baker Board were commonly held. It reported that ". . . the limitations of the airplane show that the idea that aviation, acting alone, can control sea lanes, or defend the coast, or produce decisive results are visionary, as is the idea that a very large and independent air force is necessary to defend our country against air attack". Doolittle, however, supported the "visionary" Billy Mitchell in his advocacy of air power, to the extent that he appended a minority report to the Baker Board's, stating that ". . . he was convinced that the required air force can be more rapidly organised, equipped and trained if it is completely separated and developed as an entirely separate arm ...".

In 1940, Doolittle was recalled as a major and worked on converting the motor car industry to aircraft production. However, in 1942 he undertook a mission which was to make him virtually a legend in his own lifetime. A daring and imaginative plan had been drawn up involving the use of medium bombers from an aircraft carrier to raid Tokyo. Primary aim of the operation was to inflict material and psychological damage; but it would also, in part, avenge Pearl Harbour.

[1]Quoted in *Airborne to Battle: A History of Airborne Warfare 1918-1971,* by Col M. Tugwell; William Kimber, 1971.

General Arnold, the American Chief of Air Staff, knew that to lead such a mission he would require a man of exceptional skills, technically, operationally and as a commander of men: he selected James Doolittle. While the volunteer crews underwent a thorough training and preparation programme, Doolittle ensured that the aircraft, North American B-25s, were as operationally sound as possible, re-equipping them to suit the task in hand and introducing such ingenious devices as dummy guns, fitted in the tail-cone, to discourage attack from the rear.

The attack was made on April 18, 1942, Doolittle himself piloting the first of the 16 aircraft to take off from USS *Hornet*. As a result of its success the Japanese offensive was hindered, four fighter groups which could have been employed in the South Pacific being retained in Japan during 1942-43. American morale was also boosted significantly. For this operation Doolittle received the Congressional Medal of Honor.

Later in 1942 he was appointed to command the Twelfth Air Force which had been created specially for Operation *Torch,* the Anglo-US landing in North Africa; and in February 1943, when the Mediterranean Air Command came into being, was made Commander of the North-west African Strategic Air Force. The British and American

Lieutenant-General James H. Doolittle

strategic bombers operating under his command behind enemy lines contributed significantly to Allied operations in the Mediterranean and to the success of their co-operative efforts.

With the invasion of north-west Europe scheduled for mid-1944, the necessary air planning seemed beset with irreconcilable difficulties, the Transportation Plan being a central issue. In the early stages Doolittle, now commanding the Eighth Air Force in the UK, had considered this plan to be a waste of effort; but once it was adopted he provided for the integration of his heavy bombers into the overall pattern of air operations which prepared for and supported the invasion.

During the closing months of the war the Eighth Air Force was transferred to the Pacific theatre, under Doolittle's command, but before its B-29s could become operational the atomic bombs ended the war against Japan.

General Carl Spaatz Commander of the United States Strategic Air Forces in Europe from January 1, 1944. In 1940, Spaatz had been an official observer in London and had witnessed at first hand the weight of a Luftwaffe onslaught during the Battle of Britain. After Pearl Harbour and the entry of the United States into the war he became Chief of the Air Force Combat Command; then, in March 1942, Commanding General of the Eighth Air Force. The Americans anticipated a major assault on north-west Europe in 1943 and Spaatz's units were transferred to the UK as part of the Allied build-up. The heavy bombers were soon in action: the first B-17 Flying Fortress had landed at Prestwick on July 1, 1942, and within six weeks operations commenced with an attack against a marshalling yard outside Rouen. Two days later, on August 19, during the Dieppe Raid, Fortresses escorted by Spitfires paralysed the fighter station at Abbeville-Drucat for two critical hours.[1] Described officially as a reconnaissance in force, the raid furnished useful lessons for the future in the problem of invading a well-defended coast-line.

A general policy was formally agreed between the Americans and the British in September, whereby raids against Germany would be conducted at night by RAF Bomber Command and during the day by the Eighth Air Force. The latter operations were not, however, initiated until January 27, 1943, when Wilhelmshaven was attacked. From August 1942 to February 1943 a total of 2,155 tons of bombs were dropped—a small amount in comparison with the figures of the months to come—but the Air Staff was nonetheless impressed by the high-level precision bombing of Spaatz's Fortresses and Liberators.[1]

While activity was increasing in the UK, events in North Africa were taking a dramatic course, Montgomery's El Alamein offensive being followed by the Allied *Torch* landings in North Africa. The impressive pattern of co-operation and assistance by the air forces was, however, hindered by the lack of an overall air commander. In December 1942, Spaatz was detached temporarily from the Eighth Air Force to become Deputy for air operations in that theatre, with the task of co-ordinating the operations of the Eastern Air Command and the Twelfth Air Force; but although he was, in Tedder's words, able to perform "a useful function of co-ordination"[2] this did not go far enough for the British

---

[1]*Royal Air Force 1939-1945,* by Hilary St George Saunders and Denis Richards; HMSO, 1954.

[2]*With Prejudice,* by Lord Tedder; Cassell, 1966.

commander. Ultimately Tedder's views were to prevail with the formation of the Mediterranean Air Command in February 1943. Under this truly Allied organisation Spaatz was appointed Commander of the North-west African Air Forces, with the British Air Vice-Marshal Robb as his Deputy, and in this capacity he witnessed the successful Allied drive through Tunisia, into Sicily and up through Italy.

Towards the close of 1943, planning for *Overlord* gathered momentum, with many of the successful commanders from the Mediterranean being appointed to key posts.

Spaatz became Commander of the United States Strategic Air Forces in Europe (USSAFE) under a directive which was to provide for co-ordination of strategic bombing operations by the Eighth Air Force in the UK and the Fifteenth Air Force in Italy, and to bring them within the aegis of the *Overlord* command. This last point was, however, to involve him in a conflict of ideas and personality. At a time when the strength of his forces was increasing, he maintained that the most effective way that they could aid *Overlord* would be to pursue the strategic objectives of the combined bomber offensive as outlined in the *Pointblank* directive: in so doing they would need complete freedom of action and control. These opinions (though shared by Harris, the RAF Bomber Command C-in-C) were diametrically opposed to those of Leigh-Mallory, AEAF C-in-C, and, more importantly, of Tedder.

In addition to this difference in operational considerations, Spaatz, like Harris, refused to co-operate with Leigh-Mallory in any way. On one crucial question, however, the views of the two *strategic* air commanders diverged radically. Harris firmly advocated the continuation of area bombing, whereas Spaatz devised a plan which adapted the American interpretation of the *Pointblank* directive to suit the needs of *Overlord.* Known as the Oil Plan, it was issued on March 5, 1944, and centred upon attacks against oil installations, a key factor in Germany's war economy. These attacks would not only damage her resources but also force the Luftwaffe into the air in defence of this crucial resource.

The potential of this scheme was indisputable, but it was eventually rejected in favour of Leigh-Mallory's Transportation Plan when economic experts confirmed that its effects would not be felt in time to benefit significantly the opening, critical phases of the invasion.

In the three months of April, May and June, 1944, the Eighth Air Force was to drop 109,101 tons of bombs in a strenuous effort which was to include direct tactical support for the armies and assault on the V-weapon sites. Nevertheless, Spaatz's views were not basically altered, and on June 28 he wrote to Eisenhower complaining about what he considered to be misuse of the strategic air forces and suggesting that long-range operations might be resumed.

No immediate formal change in policy resulted but in fact a limited oil offensive had already begun, even before D-day. In April the Fifteenth Air Force had accomplished missions against the Ploesti oil installations, and from May the Eighth Air Force joined in similar operations. Between June and September the latter was to make six major attacks on 32 oil plants and refineries, while the 15th raided 41 in an almost continuous assault. The results of these raids, coupled with Spaatz's deep commitment, convinced the Air Staff of their long-term potential, and directives issued from September 1944 gave priority to oil targets, with communications second.

Thus in the closing months of the war Spaatz's mighty force was to strike heavily and repeatedly against these specific points and German cities.

Spaatz meanwhile was transferred to the headquarters of the Army Air Force, and in July 1945 was sent to the Pacific. The last, terrible action of the war was to be carried out under his command, for within the strategic forces he controlled were the aircraft that dropped the atomic bombs on Hiroshima and Nagasaki—attacks which vindicated the claims of the bomber proponents as to their war-winning capability.

British Air Commanders

Air Chief Marshal Sir Arthur Tedder Deputy Supreme Commander for *Overlord.* On April 15, 1944, a critical stage was reached in the air contribution to *Overlord,* with the co-ordination of all Allied strategic and tactical operations coming under the direction of the Deputy Supreme Commander, Air Chief Marshal Sir Arthur Tedder. This unifying of control accorded well with Tedder's own views on the most effective use of air power, but its achievement had made strong demands on his skills of steady reasoning and diplomacy.

Churchill had nominated Tedder as General Eisenhower's deputy in recognition of "the great part air will play in this operation". The air marshal had taken up his appointment on January 20, 1944, bringing with him a wealth of command experience.

In 1941, after a period as Deputy, he had become Air Officer Commanding-in-Chief, RAF Middle East. The tensions and demands of inter-Service co-operation were quickly apparent in the changing fortunes of that theatre, but he was particularly successful in the relationship he built up with the Army commanders.

The loss of Greece and Crete in mid-1941 demonstrated conclusively that supremacy and command of the air were vital elements in a surface campaign, for the Germans' strength had lain in their ability to conduct air operations freely from a ring of airfields surrounding the assault area. Tedder regarded the achievement of these two conditions to be the air force's most urgent task, having priority over the direct support of land and sea operations. The wisdom of this policy became apparent during Montgomery's El Alamein offensive in October 1942, when effective air superiority had permitted constant attacks on Rommel's supply routes, leaving him acutely short of fuel; enemy fighters had been subjected to a fierce offensive against them from October 9; and an elaborate programme of deception measures had been greatly assisted by the enemy's inability to make full aerial reconnaissance.

Following the Casablanca Conference in January 1943, Tedder was appointed Commander-in-Chief of the new Mediterranean Air Command, with responsibility for all the Allied air operations. Working in close co-operation with General Eisenhower, Supreme Commander for *Torch* (the Allied invasion of North Africa) and the ensuing campaigns, he aimed at effecting a complete integration of air/land/sea operations. Events in the Middle East had proved beyond doubt the indispensability of mastery of the air, while isolation of the battle area had afforded considerable tactical advantage. Tedder therefore preceded the Allied invasions of Tunisa, Sicily and Italy during 1943 with concentrated assaults on Axis air strength and with long-range strategic bombing of communications. Thus, for the invasion of Sicily, when the Allies were to use airborne troops for the first time, not one of the enemy airfields on the island was fully operational.

A technique of close support was also developed. Known as 'Tedder's carpet', it involved intensive bombing of enemy forces immediately in front of the Allied army. Although it played a significant part in the landings at Salerno in 1943, Tedder viewed it warily, fearing the Army might become too dependent on it.

In the wake of these successful operations, his appointment as Deputy Supreme Commander for *Overlord* was described as "a worthy recognition of brilliant qualities," giving "universal confidence". His relationship with Eisenhower was well-tried and based on mutual respect, while many of his subordinate commanders, including Montgomery, Brereton, Coningham and Admiral Ramsay, were familiar faces from recent campaigns.

Once more Tedder saw the total integration of the American and British Services as a pre-requisite for success. He was, however, confronted with profound problems in the air forces, concerning primarily the command and role of the strategic bombers.

In making his nomination Churchill opined that "Tedder with his unique experience and close relationship as Deputy to the Supreme Commander ought to be in fact and form the complete master of all air operations". This, unfortunately, conflicted with the ideas of the British Chiefs of Staff, who saw the operational requirements of *Overlord* as but part of the RAF's complex role; a unified command would not, therefore, be strictly relevant to the situation. Tedder's own views were expressed in anxious words to the Chief of the Air Staff, Sir Charles Portal, on February 22, 1944:

"As I see it, one of the main lessons of the Mediterranean campaign was not merely the advisability of, but the necessity for, unified command of the Air Force. I know this is Eisenhower's view. ... I think everybody in authority, both British and American, realises that it is going to be hard work ... to maintain harmonious co-operation during this next job. A split on the question of the control of air forces might well ... precipitate a quite irremedial cleavage."

The matter was complicated by clashes of personality. Spaatz, the commander of the USSAFE, refused to accept orders from Leigh-Mallory, Commander-in-Chief of the AEAF; while the AOC-in-C, RAF Bomber Command, Harris, was determined to follow his own path in the light of the *Pointblank* directive.

The eventual compromise solution, reached on March 22, was to tax Tedder's personal resources still further, for it was agreed that direction of the strategic air forces would pass to the Supreme Commander *when* a plan for air support of *Overlord* had been approved by Eisenhower and Portal. On February 29 the Supreme Commander had instructed Tedder to take charge of air planning, in view of the impasse reached by Leigh-Mallory's informal committee which had been endeavouring to co-ordinate the ideas of the tactical and strategic commanders. In taking this step Tedder was assured of Eisenhower's full practical support.

The conclusions which Tedder came to were based not on any national, service or command rivalry, but on factual evidence and an appreciation of the particular situation in relation to the resources available. He firmly believed that "... concentration against one common (target) system, by both day and night, is essential". His experience in previous commands pointed to the adoption of Leigh-Mallory's Transportation Plan, which aimed at the attainment of air superiority and at a concentrated assault on enemy communications directly affecting the opening phase of the invasion. Such an undertaking, if fully implemented, would require the co-ordination of *all* the Allied air forces and would not only effectively isolate the battle area but could benefit further offensives by dislocating the entire railway network of German-held Europe.

The advantages of this plan, as thoroughly demonstrated by Tedder, overcame the objections and alternatives put forward by the strategic air commanders. Harris's assertions that Bomber Command would be incapable of executing the precision attacks demanded by the plan were invalidated when the RAF strategic bombers successfully attacked the railway centre at Trappes in a series of experimental raids ordered by Air Chief Marshal Sir Charles Portal in March; while expert opinion showed that the effects of Spaatz's oil plan could not be immediate enough to be of positive value to the opening ground campaign.

Tedder's recommendation of the Transportation Plan was accepted by Eisenhower and Portal, but further problems arose when opposition by the War Cabinet—based largely on a fear of the political repercussions that might follow high civilian casualties—put final approval in jeopardy. Attempts at modifying the list of targets, coupled with the production of actual casualty figures, did little to resolve the situation. However, on April 14 overall direction of the Allied air forces had been conferred on the Supreme Commander, who in turn passed the immediate responsibility to his Deputy. With these powers, and aware of the danger of any further delay in initiating the full assault, Tedder decided to approve the issue of a directive to Spaatz and Harris, with the proviso that the political aspects of the plan would be kept under continuous supervision.

Tedder's readiness to act as a situation demanded was evident again later that month, when execution of the plan was still being held up. Despite the rejection of the oil plan as the primary pattern of attack, he agreed to the bombing of certain oil targets by Spaatz's aircraft, to draw the Luftwaffe into combat. In similar spirit, when the carefully prepared Transportation Plan finally got under way, he specifically instructed the bomber commanders to watch the enemy closely and to strike at the railway system as it was being used, not simply in accordance with the plan as written.

Four months after the invasion began, control of the strategic air forces reverted to the Combined Chiefs of Staff, and Tedder took over the direction of the tactical air forces, following Leigh-Mallory's appointment to the Far East. His continued advocacy of the communications assault contributed to expansion of the plan to embrace the German homeland. This, together with the major offensive against enemy oil installations, contributed substantially to eventual German defeat.

The success of Tedder's war commands owed much to his ability to draw on experience and to adapt it to new resources and situations. The skill with which he gained the co-operation of such diverse personalities as Spaatz, Harris and Leigh-Mallory stemmed both from his personal tact and from the respect he commanded as a successful officer. It was these qualities that led Eisenhower to describe him as "one of the few great military leaders of our time".

Air Chief Marshal Sir Trafford Leigh-Mallory Commander-in-Chief, Allied Expeditionary Air Force. The appointment of Air Chief Marshal Sir Trafford Leigh-Mallory, AOC-in-C, RAF Fighter Command, to the post of Commander-in-Chief of the Allied Expeditionary Air Force was agreed at the Quebec Conference in August 1943. The decision was made in the light of current planning which, in the view of Sir Charles Portal, suggested that the most important aspect of the air contribution to *Overlord* would be the attainment of superiority over the beachheads[1]. The choice of the fighter commander therefore seemed appropriate and was accepted by the Americans.

Leigh-Mallory's career had been highly successful. Between 1927-30 he had been Commandant of the School of Army Co-operation, before being appointed to Air Staff posts. During the Battle of Britain he had commanded No 12 Group, responsible for defending the Midlands and the east coast shipping routes. Strongly critical of the tactics employed by No 11 Group's Commander, Sir Keith Park, who believed in intercepting enemy bombers on their way to the targets, he had advocated the use of the 'big wing' formation against the Luftwaffe with mass formations of fighters attacking enemy bombers, either before or after they had made their raid. At the end of 1940 he took Park's place, and under Air Chief Marshal Sir W. Sholto Douglas, who had become AOC-in-C RAF Fighter Command, switched the emphasis to the offensive, with the aim of forcing the enemy to divert some of his defensive strength from other theatres.

August 1942 saw Leigh-Mallory in control of air operations for the Dieppe landing. With a mainly fighter force, he provided outstanding protection for the ground operations. However, the heavy preponderance of fighters over bombers mitigated against effective close support for the landings, cannon fire making little impression against the concrete German defences. In addition, confusion on the ground prevented the selection of suitable targets[2]. Nonetheless, the lessons of this operation were valuable to future Allied planning. In November 1942 he succeeded Air Chief Marshal Sir W. Sholto Douglas as Air Officer Commander-in-Chief, Fighter Command, and in mid-1943—largely as a result of his proposals—the 2nd Tactical Air Force, which was to be the RAF component of the Allied Expeditionary Air Force, was formed within his Command.

The many problems which were to attend his subsequent appointment as commander of the AEAF stemmed both from circumstances and from his own personality. Difficulties experienced by the British and Americans in deciding the exact nature of the Air Commander-in-Chief's powers were aggravated by the delay in appointing a Supreme Commander. When Leigh-Mallory's directive was finally issued on November 16, 1943, it defined his command of the tactical air forces allotted to *Overlord* but informed him that "directives for the control of the Strategic Air Forces will follow at a later date". Thus his exact position was still unclear when he began formulating the air plans which were to provoke much debate.

The situation was further complicated by his personality. Leigh-Mallory has been variously described as "aggressive", "bluff", "forceful", "dogmatic"—qualities which were hardly likely to foster easy relationships, particularly when those with whom he was to work were equally "bluff". The loyalty and confidence he inspired in his staff and

[1] *The Strategic Air Offensive Against Germany 1939-1945,* by Sir Charles Webster and Noble Frankland; HMSO, 1961.
[2] *Royal Air Force 1939-1945,* by Hilary St George Saunders and Denis Richards; HMSO, 1954.

fighting squadrons were not shared by the Prime Minister or Eisenhower, neither of whom would accept him as *overall* air commander. Furthermore, as the air involvement in *Overlord* developed and expanded, the choice of a fighter commander without strategic experience became less appropriate.[1] Few could question Leigh-Mallory's success in a tactical role but he had no experience of heavy bomber operations.

Meanwhile, he set about the task of preparing with the commanders of the other two Services a plan for the assault and seizure of a bridgehead in Normandy and for its enlargement into a lodgement area. On February 1, 1944, the *Neptune* initial joint plan was issued, from which each Service was to draw up its detailed plan; Leigh-Mallory's overall air plan was issued on April 15.

Probably his most valuable contribution to the success of *Overlord* was his Transportation Plan, aimed at attaining air superiority and at co-ordinating an assault on enemy communications directly affecting the opening phase of the invasion. This was developed in collaboration with the 21st Army Group and expert advisers, including Professor S. Zuckerman, who had been involved in planning the Allied attack on the Italian railway system, and R. E. Brant, an expert on the French railway network. The plan was firmly supported by Tedder, who advocated the total co-ordination of Allied air strength in an all-out attack on a common target system. Indeed, eventual adoption of the plan, in view of the personal animosity and practical opposition of the two strategic air commanders, Spaatz and Harris, and the political qualms of the British War Cabinet, would have been in some doubt if Leigh-Mallory had had to defend it alone.

The success of *Neptune* was essential to the Allies, and attention to detail, while considering the grand design, was vital. Thus Leigh-Mallory's opposition to the dropping of the 82nd and 101st US Airborne Divisions, when the hazards of the operation appeared great, was amply justified. That his objection was over-ruled by Eisenhower was due to the necessity of this operation for the capture of *Utah* beach. With the decision made, the Air Commander endeavoured to enhance the success of the operation with meticulous planning and rehearsal. Again, the anxiety he was to express about weather conditions in the final meetings to decide the date of D-day was prompted as much by his consideration of the operational needs of his aircraft as by what has been termed "pessimism".

Leigh-Mallory had enjoyed the full support of Tedder in regard to the Transportation Plan, but on certain important issues their views diverged. In his autobiography *With Prejudice*,[2] Tedder commented that ". . . Leigh-Mallory's weakness was his desire to interfere with subordinate commanders". And as the invasion continued he was impelled to tell him that ". . . his job was not to command but to command in chief . . .". Moreover, Tedder did not agree with Leigh-Mallory's overt preference for road and rail targets, in direct support of the army, at the expense of the airfield targets being advocated forcefully by the Americans. He felt that neither Leigh-Mallory nor the Army appreciated the limitations of air support in the battlefield or the full scope of air power outside the battle area.

In spite of the personal clashes that marked Leigh-Mallory's period as commander of the AEAF, the fact remains that his contribution to the planning and execution of Allied

[1] *The Strategic Air Offensive Against Germany 1939-1945*, Sir Charles Webster and N. Frankland. See also *Forged in Fire*, by DeWitt S. Copp (Doubleday & Co., 1982): "Sir Winston was no more enamored of the idea of Leigh-Mallory dictating bombing policy than was Spaatz, since the Air Chief Marshal had spent all his time in fighters".

[2] Cassell & Co., 1966.

air operations was instrumental to the success of *Overlord*.

In November 1944 he was appointed Commander-in-Chief, South-East Asia, but was killed in an air crash on his way to take up the post.

Air Marshal Sir Arthur Coningham Commander, British Second Tactical Air Force.

Early in the war Arthur 'Mary' (i.e. 'Maori', a reference to his New Zealand nationality) Coningham commanded No 4 Bomber Group at York. In July 1941 he was appointed Commander of the Western Desert Air Force which formed part of the Middle East Command under Tedder. His views on the role and potential of the air arm coincided largely with those of his C-in-C. Like Tedder he believed that the air force had an independent role to play, over and above the immediate support of the other two Services; however, when such support was to be provided, overall control of the squadrons involved should remain essentially with the air commanders who would work in close collaboration with their army and naval counterparts.

Again in common with Tedder, he recognised the enormous benefits to be derived from inter-Service co-operation, and immediately on taking up his command set about establishing close links with the Army. A particularly successful relationship was achieved with General Ritchie, who replaced General Cunningham at the head of the Eighth Army during the *Crusader* offensive, and this policy was continued when General Montgomery took over command in August 1942, prior to the final desert operations.

Air superiority was to prove a key factor in British, then Allied, success in North Africa and Coningham's squadrons contributed significantly to this, despite problems of reinforcements and the demands of other theatres. Before the *Crusader* operations in November 1941, and Montgomery's El Alamein offensive in October 1942, concentrated attacks were made against Axis air strength and its supply routes, with the result that during its push westwards the Army had greater freedom to manoeuvre while the Air Force was able both to protect and to complement the surface operations. Equally important, Coningham's aircraft had been able to maintain their air superiority when the Army was on the defensive, as in May 1942, when Rommel resumed his offensive with an attack on the Gazala line; moreover, the close support and cover afforded to the Army was augmented by a campaign of continual harrassment of the Luftwaffe, including attacks on newly occupied landing grounds.

Coningham's approach to his command was thorough and far-sighted. Collaborating with Tedder and his fellow officers, he moulded the Western Desert Air Force into a highly mobile and efficient organisation, well-suited to the conditions and fluidity of desert warefare.

With the formation of the Mediterranean Air Command at the beginning of 1943, he was appointed Commander of the Allied North-west African Tactical Air Force. A major aim of those planning the coming operations was to establish the closest possible co-operation between the Allied commanders of all three Services; and Coningham's achievements in the Western Desert, working as he had been with American units from mid-1942, well qualified him for the task. The pattern of close co-operation was to be successfully repeated: the joint headquarters of Coningham and General Alexander worked well, and the ensuing air assault against enemy communications, supplies and air strength assisted and supplemented the surface action, with the Allied advance through

Tunisia followed in July 1943 by the invasion first of Sicily and then, two months later, of Italy.

In common with many of the successful Commanders from the Mediterranean theatre, Coningham was to turn his attention to north-west Europe at the beginning of 1944. In addition to assuming command of the Second Tactical Air Force he was made responsible by Leigh-Mallory for the operational planning and control of the Advanced Allied Expeditionary Air Force up to, and including, the opening phase of *Overlord*. In this capacity he was to work closely with Montgomery, who was to command all the Allied ground forces over the same period. Accordingly, Coningham's headquarters at Uxbridge was staffed jointly by American and RAF officers and by representatives of the 21st Army Group.

The enormous effort expended by the tactical air forces prior to D-day, in transportation attacks, in reconnaissance and in obliterating German radar and radio installations, contributed to the comparative smoothness of the actual invasion. Indeed it was Coningham who put forward the idea of using fighter-bombers to destroy the difficult bridge targets over the Seine. During the weeks following the initial landings the Second Tactical Air Force's main task was to attack transport and airfields while the American Ninth Air Force held the Luftwaffe at bay; but German air strength had been so severely hit that Luftwaffe operations were seriously limited.

On August 1 Coningham moved to France, setting up his main headquarters adjacent to those of the 21st Army Group, and during the last year of the war saw the activities of his aircraft steadily grow to cover all the skies of Western Europe.

Coningham's tactical skill during the war years was fostered and developed by his own originality, courage and capability and by the foresight of Tedder, who allowed him a certain degree of latitude. Tedder was, however, occasionally obliged to intervene—as in April 1943 when he ordered Coningham to withdraw and formally apologise for an abrupt signal which had been sent to General Patton in response to apparent criticism of certain air operations.

Although he generally adhered to the policy of inter-service co-operation, instances arose when Coningham became sharply critical. Thus, at the end of June 1944, he joined with Leigh-Mallory in demanding that Montgomery comply with the original plan to secure airfields south-east of Caen. The Army Commander believed that the requirements of his troops could now be met sufficiently by the air forces as they were currently placed. Coningham's evaluation of this attitude largely sums up the approach he adopted throughout his career; for he considered that it virtually relegated the air force to an auxiliary status, grossly under-estimating the complex role it was capable of performing.

Air Chief Marshal Sir Arthur T. Harris, AOC-in-C, RAF Bomber Command. A South African by birth, Arthur Harris proved a distinguished pilot in the 1914-18 War and had held a succession of increasingly important appointments during the 1920s and '30s. These included squadron commander in India, Iraq and the UK; head of the Air Ministry Plans Branch; and AOC RAF Palestine and Transjordan; in 1939 he commanded No 5 Bomber Group. In 1941, following a period as Deputy Chief of the Air Staff, he headed a Royal Air Force delegation to Washington to discuss air co-operation. On his return he was appointed Air Officer Commanding-in-Chief, Bomber Command, in February 1942.

The force he took over was in urgent need of someone of his positive and aggressive spirit to lift its wilting morale; operations had been proving costly and results disappointing, while the flow of new aircraft had been slow. Harris immediately set out to inspire a fresh confidence among his squadrons.

Immediate plans were made to step up the offensive. A few days before he took up his appointment, a directive had been issued to Bomber Command naming the four industrial areas around Essen, Duisberg, Dusseldorf and Cologne as primary targets for bombing raids, and ordering operations to be "focussed on the morale of the enemy civil population and, in particular, of the industrial workers". Harris had by now abandoned a previously held belief in precision bombing and in essence this directive (which had been personally endorsed by Air Chief Marshal Sir Charles Portal), i.e. area bombing, was to become his unfaltering creed in the coming months. The early raids on the Ruhr proved only partially successful, but encouraging results were obtained at Lübeck and Rostock. However, the spectacular was to be achieved on May 30, 1942, when the 'Thousand Bomber' raid on Cologne wrought havoc at relatively small cost. Similar raids on Essen and Bremen were to follow but with less success.

In general, Harris tended to view new ideas and techniques with scepticism. He opposed the use of incendiary bombs in favour of the 4,000 and 8,000lb high-explosive bombs; he feared that the formation of the Pathfinder force would create an élite body, detrimental to general squadron morale; he had spoken against the development of the 'Dambuster' bombs. Moreover, his single-minded adherence to the policy of area bombing dictated totally his interpretation of the directive relating to the combined bomber offensive in 1943. The final document stated that the purpose of the air war against Germany should be "to bring about the progressive destruction and dislocation of the German military, industrial and economic system and the undermining of the morale of the German people to a point where their capacity for armed resistance is fatally weakened. This is construed as meaning so weakened as to permit initiation of final combined operations on the Continent". The resulting divergence in interpretation of this statement by the Allied commanders has been related in the opening chapter, but for Harris, the clause relating to the undermining of German morale assumed the greatest importance, coinciding so exactly with his own ideas, and he directed Bomber Command's operations accordingly. The tremendous damage and destruction inflicted during the raids on the Ruhr, on Hamburg and on Berlin owed much to the courage and tenacity Harris inspired in his crews, but the morale of the German people was to prove remarkably resilient and their industries continued. In fact, fighter production increased during 1944, despite the priority afforded to attacks on it in the *Pointblank* directive. On this point it is significant that between June 10, 1943, and March 25, 1944, of the 58 major attacks[1] made by Bomber Command on German cities and industrial targets, few save Kassel were important centres of aircraft production although all manufactured essential parts[2]. Weather and operational difficulties were partly responsible for this record but Harris's unshakeable faith in area bombing also contributed.

He rejected what he termed 'panacea' targets—specific targets which were vital to a sector of the German industrial or economic structure. It was this attitude, indeed, which

[1] i.e., attacks made by 400 aircraft or more.
[2] *Royal Air Force 1939-1945,* by Hilary St George Saunders and Denis Richards; HMSO, 1954.

prompted the Air Staff to issue a directive on January 14, 1944, urging him to ". . . adhere to the spirit of the *(Pointblank)* directive . . ." and instructing him, in particular, to attack the Schweinfurt ball-bearing factories. Up to that point, he had resisted this target, considering it potentially hazardous and costly to attack. In obedience to the order the raid was executed on 24/25 February, achieving little permanent success.

Meanwhile Harris was fighting for his beliefs in the planning for the seemingly "inescapable commitment" of *Overlord*. Like Spaatz, he was convinced of the ability of the strategic offensive to defeat Germany, but he differed from his American counterpart in detail, for the latter advocated the bombing of specific targets in the German oil industry—another 'panacea' policy as far as Harris was concerned. In January, 1944 he stated: "The only efficient support which Bomber Command can give to *Overlord* is the intensification of attacks on suitable industrial centres in Germany as and when opportunity offers. If we attempt to substitute for this process attacks on gun emplacements, beach defences, communications or dumps in occupied territory, we shall commit the irremediable error of diverting our best weapon from the military function for which it has been equipped and trained to tasks which it cannot effectively carry out".

The extent of the British bomber commander's opposition extended beyond planning; personalities were also involved, in particular Leigh-Mallory, whom Harris virtually ignored.

Obstinacy, forcefulness, single-mindedness are characteristics frequently applied to him, but another should be added to the list—loyalty. In the face of the determination of the *Overlord* commanders, and especially with the reasoning and tact of the Deputy Supreme Commander, Tedder, he witnessed the forfeiture of the independence of the strategic air forces, albeit temporarily, so that they might be used in a plan in which he did not believe. In addition, he was obliged to accept techniques and skills which he had argued vehemently to be outside the range of his bomber crews: in the early months of 1944 Tedder required the strategic bombers to attack railway marshalling yards and repair depots as part of his pre-invasion bombing programme. Harris naturally objected to this both on the grounds of diverting his bombers away from the night-time area offensive over Germany and because he considered his crews incapable of executing day or night precision attacks. He was, however, ordered to direct six experimental night-time attacks on marshalling yards in France, beginning at Trappes. The outstanding success of these raids confirmed Bomber Command's role in the preparations for the Allied invasion and its C-in-C committed his squadrons to perform to the best of their ability the tasks allotted to it by the *Overlord* command.

But dissension was not to end here. Following the success of the opening phases of the invasion, control of the strategic air forces reverted to the Combined Chiefs of Staff. A directive was issued subsequently, on September 25, 1944, listing oil targets as first priority, with communications second. Harris's view on 'panacea' targets had not altered: of the 61,204 tons of bombs dropped by Bomber Command in October only 3,653 tons or 6 per cent were aimed at oil installations. The inevitable conflict of opinion which arose involved Portal, as Chief of the Air Staff, and Harris in a confrontation of increasing seriousness. In November the percentage of attacks against oil targets increased to 24.6 per cent of the total tonnage, but by the end of December the tide had again turned. A climax was reached on January 18, 1945, when Harris suggested that he should resign his command. Portal realised that such a course was out of the question; it would not only cause a scandal but would irreparably harm the morale of Bomber Command, whose all-out support was still urgently needed. What is more, the great and courageous achievements of the Command could not be ignored. In his reply Portal wrote: ". . . We must wait until the end of the war before we can know for certain who was right, and I sincerely hope that until then you will continue in command of the force which has done so much towards defeating the enemy and has brought such credit and renown to yourself and to the Air Force."

The peak of Bomber Command's night offensive was reached with the devastating attack on Dresden on 14/15 February, 1945. After this, attention once more focussed on precision targets to speed the final collapse of Germany.

Sir Arthur Harris believed that by forcing the Germans on to the defensive, a great number of British lives had been spared. His resolution was an inspiration to those he commanded; his ruthlessness represented a total commitment to winning the war.

German Air Commanders

Generalmajor Dietrich Peltz, Commander Fliegerkorps IX. Described by one of his former RAF opponents[1] as "a young, pugnacious and distinguished officer", Peltz was transferred from Italy in August 1943 and given command of Fliegerkorps IX, which controlled all the Luftwaffe long-range bomber units based in northern France and the Low Countries. At the same time Fliegerkorps IX was reinforced by the whole of the long-range bomber force from Italy, withdrawn to the west. Early in 1944, Peltz was to have the uneasy honour of launching the last German manned bomber offensive of World War II against England. Hence the title conferred on him by Göring—"Angriffsführer England" (leader of the assault on England)—after retaliation by the Luftwaffe had been decided upon, following the destruction of Hamburg by RAF Bomber Command in July 1943.

Just before the war, and in the campaign against Poland with which it opened, Peltz had commanded dive-bomber and bomber units. During the 1940-41 Luftwaffe offensive against England he held similar commands. Subsequently he had a staff appointment concerned with the inspection of bombers and organisation of the bomber arm. He used his experience of ground-attack operations to good effect against the Allies in the Mediterranean theatre, and from March 1943 he was responsible for a dive-bomber formation leaders' course in Foggia, Italy. A major-general by the age of 29, Peltz was initially responsible, after taking command of Fliegerkorps IX, for the low-level surprise attacks by fighter-bombers against English south coast towns.

His plans for a bomber offensive against the United Kingdom turned mainly on the building-up of Fliegerkorps IX strength through reinforcement from Italy, and on an improvement in the standard of aircrew training. Aircraft strength was brought up to about 550—chiefly Junkers Ju88s and Ju188s (the latter a developed version of the former) and Dornier Do17s. In addition, there were about 35 of the new Heinkel He177s,

[1] AVM J. E. ('Johnnie') Johnson, in *Full Circle: The Story of Air Fighting* (Chatto and Windus, 1964).

the unsuccessful heavy bomber developed by Germany during the war, and some 20 Messerschmitt Me410 and 25 Focke-Wulf FW190 fighters pressed into bombing service. In order to improve aircrew skill, Peltz introduced specialist pathfinder units on the lines of the RAF Bomber Command PFF squadrons.

The offensive which Fliegerkorps IX launched on January 21, 1944, with an attack on London represented the reprisal which Hitler had ordered after the destruction of Hamburg. The first attack was succeeded by a second on January 29; others followed, with the final raid on April 18; there were also attacks upon Hull and Bristol, but despite the damage caused the offensive had no significant effect upon British morale.

A last bold stroke by Peltz against the Allies was made on January 1, 1945, when he sent about 800 fighters and fighter-bombers across the Rhine in support of von Runstedt after the Ardennes offensive; but as with his bomber operations, lack of training and experience among the pilots offset the element of surprise. About 200 aircraft were lost and this late blow by the almost-defeated Luftwaffe failed to hold up the Allied advance.

Generalfeldmarschall Hugo Sperrle As Commander-in-Chief of Luftflotte 3 in France and Belgium, Sperrle controlled the Luftwaffe formation directly confronting the Allied air forces which were supporting the Normandy landings. Aged 59, he had commanded Luftflotte 3 since before the war when he was appointed Commander West. Joint leader with Kesselring of Luftwaffe forces in the Battle of Britain, his bombers had been responsible for the 1940 night attacks on the UK. Originally, however, he had been opposed to the bombing of towns by the Luftwaffe; one reason he gave for this was that a bomb might hit the US Embassy in Paris, for example, and bring the Americans into the war on the side of Britain and France. Since, by 1944, he had to face the full weight of an Anglo-American air offensive, his early fears about United States intervention were amply justified.

Reichsmarschall Herman Göring, C-in-C Luftwaffe, harangues some of his aircrew.

Generalleutnant Adolf Galland, Inspector of Fighters from the end of 1941 (wearing white jacket), with some of his pilots.

Generalfeldmarschall Kesselring

Generalfeldmarschall Hugo Sperrle

Sperrle had made no distinguished or original contribution to military aviation and was said to have greater talents as a bully than as a strategist or planner. As the son of a publican in Ludwigsburg, Bavaria, he had been unable to become a cadet in the officer corps in his home town and had to begin his Army career abroad in Strasburg, with the 126th Bavarian Infantry Regiment stationed there as part of the Army of Occupation. However, during World War I he became OC Aviators of an Army Group and then commanded the air units of the 7th Army though he was never an operational pilot.

With the re-emergence of the German Air Force under the Nazis, Sperrle became (in 1934) OC Air Division 1, then in the following year a Major-General and OC Air District 5. He was associated with the cynical Nazi deployment of air power in the Spanish Civil War, as first commander of the Condor Legion in 1936, though he later relinquished this command to General Volkmann. Promoted to Lieutenant-General in 1937, he became General of Aviators in that year and in 1938 was appointed Commander-in-Chief of Air Force Group 3[1]. His command of Luftflotte 3 dated from January 2, 1939, with headquarters in Munich. However, from the start of the war he commanded the German Air Force in the West, when in the "blitzkrieg" of 1940 it supported the victorious Army; and in that year he was promoted to Generalfeldmarschall. As C-in-C of Luftflotte 3 he reportedly delegated most of the operational planning to his Chief of Staff and right-hand man, Günther Korten.

Generalleutnant Adolf Galland General der Jagdflieger until January 1945, when he was removed for political reasons by Göring.

His wartime career was one of the most dramatic and successful in the Luftwaffe. He achieved one of its highest ranks and gained its most coveted decoration, the Oak Leaves with Swords and Diamonds to the Knight's Cross of the Iron Cross. Not only was he brilliant as a fighter pilot, with 104 victories to his credit against Allied aircraft, but he applied the knowledge gained in combat to improve the techniques and tactics of the Luftwaffe in air fighting. His sympathy with the pilots under his command, and his determination to stand up for them, led him into constant conflict with authority, particularly with Göring as C-in-C. It was the latter's willingness to blame the fighter arm for German failures, and his unwillingness to stand up to Hitler's hysterical demand that it should be disbanded, that led to the final conflict and Galland's dismissal as commander of the fighter arm in January, 1945.

As a fighter pilot, Galland was one of the nine top "aces" of the Luftwaffe, his operational career spanning the whole of the Second World War, from Poland in 1939 to a beleaguered Germany in 1945 and including the Battle of Britain. He was General der Jagdflieger from the end of 1941, when he succeeded Werner Mölders on the latter's death in a flying accident. When promoted to Generalmajor in 1942 at the age of 30, he was the youngest general of the German armed forces.

After his removal from high command he went back to operational flying and, though still a Lieutenant-general, commanded a squadron—Jagdverband 44, which had Messerschmitt Me262 twin-jet fighters. His fighting career ended on April 26, 1945, when he led six Me262s into action against a formation of USAAF B-26 Marauders and was himself shot down by an escorting (but unseen) P-51 Mustang. Although his aircraft was damaged, and he was injured, he managed to land on Riem airfield near Munich—an airfield under attack at the time by P-47 Thunderbolts—and survived the war.

[1]He had the distinction of being described by Hitler as "Germany's most brutal-looking general" (see *Architects of Air Power,* by David Nevin; Time-Life Books, 1981).

Key to Map

⬜ Aircraft production & industrial targets

○ Attacks on radar stations

◉ Operation Taxable

◆ Coastal Command Operations

(OIL) Bombing of oil plants

(U) Bombing of U-Boat pens

(P) Airborne forces dropping zones
↓ Glider flight paths

● Bombing Atlantic Wall defences

△ Operation Crossbow

⌒ Bombing of bridges

—■— Rail network targets

miles 0 10 20 30 40 50 60 70 80 90 100

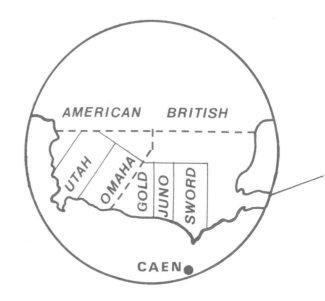

Map
of the
Overlord
Operations

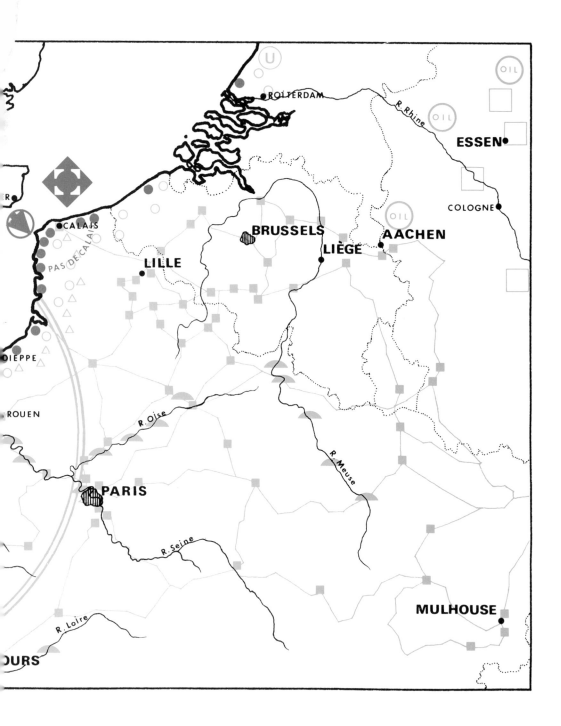

ROTTERDAM

R. Rhine

ESSEN

COLOGNE

CALAIS

PAS DE CALAIS

LILLE

BRUSSELS

LIÈGE

AACHEN

DIEPPE

ROUEN

R. Oise

R. Meuse

PARIS

R. Seine

R. Loire

MULHOUSE

OURS

97

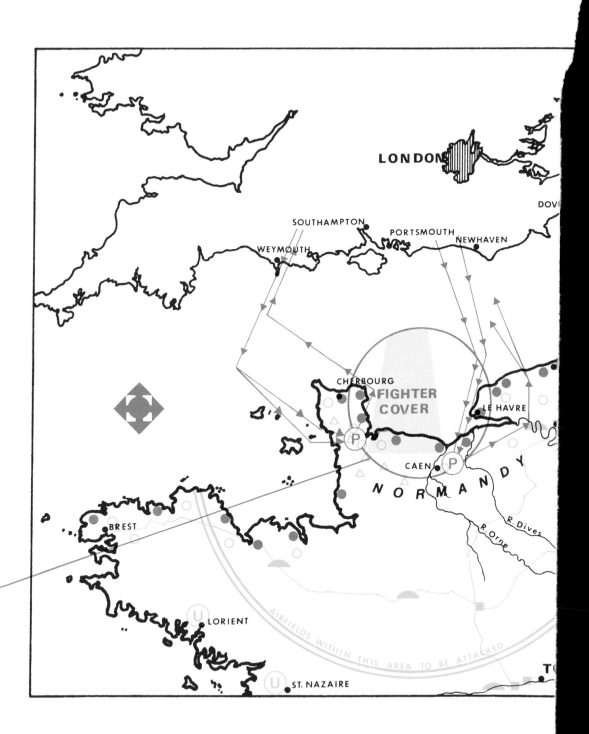

LONDON

DOV

SOUTHAMPTON

PORTSMOUTH NEWHAVEN

WEYMOUTH

CHERBOURG
FIGHTER
COVER

LE HAVRE

CAEN

N O R M A N D Y

R. Dives

R. Orne

BREST

LORIENT

AIRFIELDS WITHIN THIS AREA TO BE ATTACKED

ST. NAZAIRE

T

Chapter 5

Overlord:

The Air Assault

With his assumption of control over strategic air forces from April 14, 1944, the Supreme Commander, General Eisenhower, had under his direction the greatest concentration of air power that had ever been deployed to that time. It was all used from then on to help in the achievement of the directive he had been given by the Combined Chiefs of Staff on February 11, 1944: "You will enter the Continent of Europe and, in conjunction with the other United Nations, undertake operations aimed at the heart of Germany and the destruction of her armed forces."

The air offensive which Eisenhower thus controlled (through his Deputy Supreme Commander, Air Chief Marshal Sir Arthur Tedder) was like a mighty counterpoint to the main theme of entry into Europe by land—a counterpoint which began well before this main theme, then continued with it until victory had been won.

One strand in this counterpoint was the combined bomber offensive, authorised by the Combined Chiefs of Staff before Eisenhower came to take command of the invasion forces. This offensive had been striking at the roots of the German war economy—its aircraft and ball-bearing production, its oil and rubber supplies—and at the submarine fleet which menaced Allied shipping. Additionally, the daylight part of it, by USAAF B-17s and B-24s, had contributed significantly to the attrition of Luftwaffe fighter strength, and to the withdrawal of FW190 and Me109 squadrons from northern France, because of the successes of the American long-range Thunderbolts and Mustangs escorting the 8th Air Force bombers. These USAAF fighters, in thus extending Allied air superiority far across Europe, contributed dramatically to the eventual success of the Allied landings in Normandy.

Another strand was that which followed from Eisenhower's control of the strategic air forces—use of the Allied heavy bombers in attacks upon the communications systems on which the German armies would rely in resisting the Allied advance inland. That this tactical employment of RAF Bomber Command and USAAF 8th Air Force aircraft was a major factor in carrying through Operation *Overlord* is clear from the Supreme Commander's report to the Combined Chiefs of Staff[1] when he refers to the "communications plan":-

"By D-day the Strategic Air Forces together with the Tactical Air Forces had so successfully performed their mission of disrupting enemy communications that there was

[1]HMSO, 1946.

98

A-20s of the USAF 9th Air Force bomb a rail centre north-east of Brussels on 7 May 1944

a chronic shortage of locomotives and cars, repair facilities were inadequate, coal stocks were reduced to a six days' supply, and 74 bridges and tunnels leading to the battle area were impassable. The communications chaos thus produced had fatal effects upon the enemy's attempts at reinforcement of the threatened areas after our landings."

This decision to lay waste the railway system of northern France had political and moral implications, because the bombing would obviously cost the lives of Frenchmen when their country's liberation was so near. As Eisenhower explained:-

"The inital attacks upon the communications system in France were undertaken as the result of an extremely difficult decision for which I assumed the full responsibility. I was aware that the attacks upon the marshalling yards and rail centers, by both the Strategic and Tactical Air Forces, would prove costly in French lives. In addition, a very important part of the French economy would for a considerable period be rendered useless. On separate occasions both Prime Minister Churchill and General Koenig, Commander of the French Forces of the Interior, asked that I reconsider my decision to bomb these particular targets. General Koenig requested once that he be permitted to participate as a member of a review board to determine the relative necessity of bombing centers of population; with regard to the loss of French lives, however, he took a stern and soldierly attitude, remarking: 'It is war'."

The railway bridge at Oissel, south of Rouen, made impassable to traffic by bombing.

Damage done in these attacks was graphically described in a 'Report on the German Transport Ministry's view of Recent Air Attacks on Railways', dated May 15, 1944,[1] which said:-

"In the occupied areas of the West, particularly in Belgium and northern France, the raids carried out in recent weeks have caused systematic breakdown of all main lines; the coastal defences have been cut off from the supply bases in the interior, thus producing a situation which threatens to have serious consequences. ... Large-scale strategic movement of troops by rail is practically impossible at the present time, and must remain so while attacks are maintained at the present intensity. ... In assessing the situation as a whole it must further be borne in mind that, owing to the widespread destruction and damage of important construction and repair shops, the maintenance and overhaul of locomotives has been considerably disorganised; this causes further critical dislocation of traffic".

Airfields were also targets for the pre-*Overlord* air offensive; so were radar stations, "eyes" of the Luftwaffe. The German Air Historical Branch, as quoted by Maj L. F. Ellis in *Victory in the West*[2], said later:

[1]Quoted in *Victory in the West Vol I The Battle of Normandy,* by Maj L. F. Ellis; HMSO, 1962.
[2]See previous footnote.

"The systematic destruction of the ground organisation of the Luftwaffe, especially of the fighter airfields, was very effective just before and during the start of the invasion. Hardly a single airfield, of those intended for fighter operations, is still serviceable". The same historian also commented that "the outstanding factor both before and during the invasion was the overwhelming air superiority of the enemy". Or, as Wg Cdr Asher Lee put it in his book *The German Air Force*[1]:-

"... a force of less than 1,000 Luftwaffe aircraft was available directly to oppose the Allied landings. The Allied air forces ... were able to throw 11,000 aircraft into the battle on the opening day.

"This great numerical disparity, impressive in itself, was a mere facet of Allied air superiority. For nearly three months prior to the assault, mass air attacks had been made on Luftwaffe bases, communications and depots in France, the Low Countries and Germany. During these attacks the Luftwaffe had been compelled to be mere onlookers of the destruction of their own life's blood. Except for occasional assaults on unescorted or weakly escorted American formations, operating over Germany, the Luftwaffe fighter units had failed to protect either their own property or treasured German war factories, or army depots, batteries or vital rail, road and sea communications. Luftwaffe night fighters which had proved so effective in the defence of Germany in 1943 proved less capable of defending French invasion targets in 1944. The complicated system of aircraft reporting and ground control which had served the Luftwaffe so well over the Reich was not so easily transferable to the French coasts and to the Paris area. The British Bomber Command had its lightest casualties of the war in its night assaults on invasion targets in France and Belgium in the late spring of 1944. ...

"German single-engined day fighter squadrons, ranged to meet the invasion, were but a shadow of their former selves. Intensive blood-letting, mainly by the American 8th Air Force, had robbed the Luftwaffe of large numbers of its most experienced fighter pilots. These were urgently required to lead formations and inspire the German Air Force to fight its way through to the targets on the assault beaches. But by D-day they were nothing other than part of a huge 1943-1944 Luftwaffe obituary list. ..."

German resistance, however, could never be discounted at any stage in the war; and the cost to the Allies of the pre-*Overlord* air offensive may be gauged from the following grim statistics of operations against Germany from April 1 to June 5, 1944 (i.e. covering the period from April 14 when the Supreme Commander had control of the Strategic Air Forces):-

Command	Approx no of sorties	Approx tons of bombs dropped	Aircraft lost
Allied Exped AF:			
2nd TAF	28,600	7,000	133
Air Defence of GB	18,600		46
9th Air Force	53,800	30,700	197

[1]Duckworth, 1946.

Bomber Command:	24,600	87,200	523
8th Air Force:			
VIIIth Bomber Cmnd	37,800	69,900	763
VIIIth Fighter Cmnd	31,800	600	291[1]

In addition to the figures given in this table, more than 5,000 sorties were made during this period by aircraft of RAF Coastal Command against German shipping and U-boats.

The United States 9th Air Force and the RAF 2nd Tactical Air Force, both complete tactical air forces with fighters, fighter-bombers, medium bombers and reconnaissance aircraft, had been formed during 1943 for the express purpose of bringing air support to the Allied entry into Europe; and securing and maintaining air supremacy during the early months of 1944 was crucial to the success of the Normandy landings on June 6 that year.

What the 8th AF fighters accomplished in the attrition of Luftwaffe fighter strength when they accompanied the 8th AF heavy bombers and defended them against German attacks has already been mentioned, and cannot be too often stressed: the Thunderbolts and Mustangs led by such pilots as Col Don Blakeslee and Capts Don Gentile and John Godfrey played a crucial part in the eventual Allied liberation of Europe by establishing, during 1943 and 1944, Allied superiority in the daylight skies over Germany.

The 9th Air Force fighters and fighter-bombers attacked enemy air power at its immediate sources, the airfields in northern France, Holland and Belgium, intensifying their operations against such targets during April and May 1944. During the latter month, both the number and the weight of attacks were increased, against more airfields, their targets lying within, or adjacent to, the invasion area. The object was to neutralise all landing-grounds within 130 miles of the assault beaches, or within a strip of territory extending as far south of the French Channel coast as the distance north from it to Allied operational bases in the UK.

Thus between May 1 and June 5 thirty-six Luftwaffe airfields, from Brittany in the west to Holland in the east, were attacked by both medium bombers and fighter-bombers of the 9th Air Force, nine of them receiving particular attention: Evreux/Fauville, attacked by one group on May 8, by two on the 20th and by two more on the 22nd, dispersal areas, hangars and a fuel dump being hit; Achiet, by two groups on May 24 and two more on the 29th, the dispersal area being hit and damage caused to the taxiway and fuel dump; Beaumont le Roger, by one group on May 11 and 23, by two groups on the 22nd and three on the 24th, the dispersal area being hit and direct hits being scored on runways and perimeter track; Cormeilles en Vexin, by three groups on May 11 and 20 and by two groups on the 22nd, causing similar damage; Beauvais/Tille, bombed by one group on May 13 and two groups on the 22nd and 24th, dispersal areas and hangars being hit, craters caused in ammunition and fuel areas, bombs bursting also on runways and taxi track; Beaumont sur Oise, by one group on May 11 and 24 and by two groups on the 20th and 26th, damage being done to dispersal areas, runway and perimeter track; Abbeville/Drucat, by one group on May 13, by two on the 21st and by three on the 24th, dispersal areas being badly damaged; Denain/Prouvy, by two groups on May 20 and by two more on the 24th, buildings being destroyed and the perimeter track and landing

[1]*Victory in the West Vol I,* by Maj L. F. Ellis; HMSO, 1962.

B-17/B-24 escorter, Luftwaffe destroyer: USAAF 8th AF P-51D Mustang 'Sky Bouncer' 413568 of the 325th Fighter Sqn., 361st Fighter Group, VIII Fighter Command, based at Bottisham.

ground damaged; and Chartres, attacked by four groups on the 26th and by three on June 3, heavy damage being caused to buildings and the runway being hit.

Damage to runways, landing grounds and taxiways increased in significance as the invasion date came nearer, the Luftwaffe being given less and less time in which to carry out repairs. Not only was it becoming increasingly difficult for them to launch defensive sorties against Allied aircraft but the effects of the latter's attacks on airfields must have become demoralising and unnerving to Luftwaffe personnel. At this stage, of course, the Germans still did not know when the Allied landings might occur, nor where. The Pas de Calais area was thought the most likely, because this would give the Allied armies not only the shortest sea crossing but also the most direct route to the German border. Other views (including those of the staff of Luftflotte 3) were that Dieppe and the bay of the Seine, or the Cherbourg—Le Havre area, looked more likely.

The United States 9th Air Force also intensified its attacks on railway centres in the pre-D-day period, particularly attacking marshalling yards. Between March 1, 1944, and D-day thirty-six marshalling yards were attacked 139 times; these targets were in Belgium and northern France, comprising closely integrated portions of the rail systems in those areas: these attacks were made by the 9th Bomber Command medium bombers and by fighter-bombers. They were at their most intense between May 1 and 20; thereafter they decreased because the emphasis was then on road and rail bridge targets.

Referring to these operations under the Transportation Plan, directed for the Supreme Commander by his Deputy, Air Chief Marshal Tedder, who co-ordinated the efforts with the C-in-C of the Allied Expeditionary Air Force, Air Chief Marshal Leigh-Mallory, the last-named's one-time deputy, Major-General Hansell, has commented[1]:-

"There was lively dissent [between the commanders of the strategic air forces, Air Chief Marshal Harris and General Spaatz] as to the most profitable method of disrupting rail traffic: by attack of marshalling yards and railroad shop facilities, or by destruction of bridges. Both methods were tried. The latter proved the more effective on later examination. The overall result was satisfactory.

"The US and British strategic air forces and the medium bombers and fighter-bombers of the US 9th Air Force devoted almost all the month of May [1944] to attack of rail transportation in France.

"The interdiction of German rail movement to the Normandy area was effective. In the words of General Spaatz, the attack on German transportation 'opened the door for invasion'.

"To provide additional assurance against interference by the German Air Force, an intensive campaign was launched against nearby airfields occupied by the German Air Force. By D-day the airfields in the area nearest to Normandy had received 6,717 tons of bombs, 3,197 of which were delivered by the 9th Air Force, 2,638 by the 8th and the remaining 882 by the RAF. ..."

Significantly, the instruments of this employment of Allied air power in the Second World War, the medium bombers of the US 9th Air Force and of the RAF 2nd Tactical Air Force, were all American—as they had been in the North African campaign of 1942/43, when the Desert Air Force employed Bostons, Baltimores, Mitchells and Marauders against the Afrika Korps. With the exception of the Baltimores, exactly the

[1]*The Air Plan that defeated Hitler,* by Maj-Gen Haywood S. Hansell, Jr, USAF (Ret).

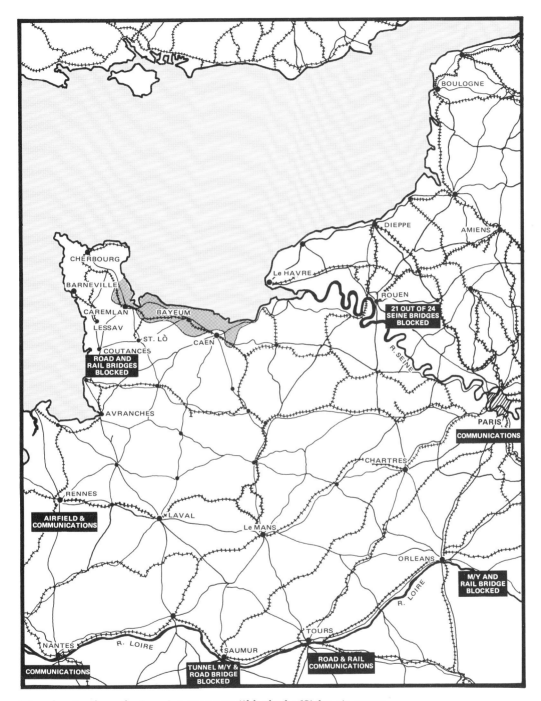

BOULOGNE

DIEPPE

AMIENS

CHERBOURG

BARNEVILLE

Le HAVRE

ROUEN

21 OUT OF 24 SEINE BRIDGES BLOCKED

CAREMLAN

BAYEUM

LESSAV

ST. LÒ

CAEN

COUTANCES

R. SEINE

ROAD AND RAIL BRIDGES BLOCKED

AVRANCHES

PARIS

COMMUNICATIONS

CHARTRES

RENNES

AIRFIELD & COMMUNICATIONS

LAVAL

Le MANS

ORLEANS

M/Y AND RAIL BRIDGE BLOCKED

R. LOIRE

TOURS

NANTES

R. LOIRE

SAUMUR

COMMUNICATIONS

TUNNEL M/Y & ROAD BRIDGE BLOCKED

ROAD & RAIL COMMUNICATIONS

Map showing how the invasion area was "blocked off" by air power

105

same types were used by the Americans, the British and their Allies in the tactical air assaults which preceded *Overlord*.

The attacks on bridges, referred to by Maj-Gen Hansell, were begun on May 7, 1944, when the Allied Expeditionary Air Force—at the instigation of Advanced Headquarters, 9th Air Force—agreed to attacks on rail bridges over the Seine and the Meuse. The same number of bridges across each river were attacked, so as not to give an indication of Allied intentions. The fighter-bombers were to concentrate on two bridges over each river and the medium bombers on one over each. Those attacked included Mantes-Gassicourt, Oissel, Orival, Vernon, Mezières, Illus, Sedan, Hirson, Mahon, Liège, Heerenthals and Hasselt. No Seine bridges were bombed between May 10 and 24, but on the latter date the attack on them was opened up, seven rail and four road bridges across the river between Paris and Rouen being attacked. On May 25, rail bridges were given priority "over all other targets, with the Seine bridges at the top of the priority", although those over the Meuse were also to continue to be attacked. The Seine road and rail bridges were especially important as targets between May 24 and D-day because of the need to isolate the battle area in Normandy, and ten rail and 14 road bridges were targets for the Allied air forces. By D-day, all the rail bridges across the Seine, from Conflans to Rouen inclusive, had been broken.

Operations by Allied fighter-bombers against railway rolling stock were aimed at supplementing the attacks on marshalling yards and bridges. The most notable in the pre-Normandy landings period was on May 21, 1944, when thirteen group missions—code-named *Chattanooga Choo-choo*—were launched against rolling stock in France north of the River Loire, eleven of them (comprising more than 500 aircraft) finding and strafing their assigned targets. Pilots claimed that 46 locomotives had been destroyed, 11 probably destroyed and 21 were damaged, while varying degrees of damage had been inflicted on 30 trains. On these missions, nine aircraft were lost.

Then on May 23 three groups—two of them operating in the Rhineland and one in northern France—strafed rolling stock, these attacks being delivered by 97 aircraft, five of which were lost. Pilots claimed that 51 locomotives had been destroyed and 14 damaged, in addition to damage inflicted on other rolling stock.

At least seven missions on June 2, 3 and 4—immediately prior to D-day—were directed against railway targets and included the bombing and strafing of trains, although claims of rolling stock destroyed were small.

The attacks on rail and road bridges, together with those on rolling stock, made during May showed what the Transportation Plan meant when put into effect, and they contributed a preamble to the more formal and fully developed interdiction programme of June and the months immediately following.

Another facet of pre-*Overlord* Allied air activities was the neutralisation, as far as possible, of the German coastal defence batteries.

Up to April 13, 1944, individual enemy batteries along the coast of northern France had been occasional targets for US 9th AF aircraft. On that date, however, an Allied Expeditionary Air Force directive instructed both the 9th AF and 2nd TAF to concentrate the necessary bombardment effort on 12 batteries which were listed, "to the end that the harassing effect of our attacks shall prevent the completion by the enemy of the construction now going on on specified targets"—that is, urgent work being

Railway yards at Turcoing under attack by Bostons of the RAF 2nd Tactical Air Force

undertaken on the coastal defences, against the threat of invasion, which the Germans knew would come but without knowing when. Two groups of six targets were defined, in each of which two were batteries under construction, the rest being completed. Nearly all the "under construction" targets lay within the invasion area, the others being as far east as Dunkirk. For security reasons (as with bridges), it was stipulated that two attacks should be made on completed batteries for each one made on a battery under construction. Similar principles were applied to later directives adding more targets.

These attacks were primarily made by medium bombers (B-26 Marauders) of the US IXth Bomber Command. Between April 13 and 30, gun positions at 24 sites were bombed, targets in two locations being attacked twice. During May, targets at 24 locations were bombed, single attacks being made on six sites, two on 12, three on three and four on two, while gun positions at Étaples were bombed six times. During the first five days of June, immediately prior to the Normandy landings, similar targets in ten localities were each attacked at least once.

The effects of these attacks on coastal batteries were hard to assess. Pilots' reports of damage caused varied greatly, and photographic evidence added little in the way of

Bridge over the River Loire destroyed by light bombers of the 9th Air Force

confirmation or otherwise. While it is certain that harassment was caused, the amount of destruction was questionable. Many guns were well hidden. In *The Longest Day,*[1] Cornelius Ryan writes that "some ... were actually in positions on the seashore itself. These were hidden in concrete emplacements beneath innocent-looking seaside homes, their barrels aimed not towards the sea but directly down the beaches. ..." In some cases, attacks failed. Ryan writes of the formidable Merville battery which was to be taken by the 9th Airborne Division on the night before the landing. A hundred Lancasters were to saturate it in advance with 4,000lb bombs; then it was to be taken by the paratroops and the glider-borne forces, "for the Merville guns could kill thousands of British troops as they touched down on *Sword* Beach". But from the start the plan misfired. "The air attack had been a complete failure; not one bomb had hit the battery. ..."[2]

Between May 15 and June 5 the USAAF reconnaissance groups were extremely active; they were concerned not only with current operations but with gathering information for the imminent landings. They also had a special role in connection with the deception and cover plan then being put into effect, that is, the carefully and elaborately organised

[1]Victor Gollancz, 1960.
[2]In *The Big Drop: The Guns of Merville, June 1944* (Jane's 1982) John Golley refers to "the hundred Lancaster bombers which had unloaded their big 'cookies' on the area of the Merville Battery, making huge craters but missing the target ... ."

Highway bridge across the River Seine at Mantes/Gassicourt, north-west of Paris, after attack by Allied Expeditionary Air Force aircraft. By cutting road and rail crossings of the Seine the AEAF hindered the movement of German reinforcements into the invasion area

simulation by the Allies of an invasion across the narrowest part of the English Channel. Thus the US 9th Air Force Tactical Reconnaissance Group planned eight missions per day in an area north of the River Seine, as part of the deception plan. Pilots were instructed to report troop movements, military concentrations and special activity on airfields and in railway marshalling yards. They were also told to report by RT on suitable fighter-bomber targets. Routes and times of entering French airspace varied from day to day, but most of the reconnaissance was over an area north of the River Somme to a depth of 100 miles from the coast.

Earlier in 1944, between February 23 and March 20, the TRG had flown 83 photographic missions to obtain Merton[1] obliques of 160 miles of French coastline and of two inshore strips, each 120 miles long. This task usually involved flying at 3,500ft on a

[1]Named after Capt John Merton, a gunnery officer at the School of Artillery, Larkhill, who invented an arbitrary grid system to which oblique photographs were matched (see *The Unseen Eye*, by Air Cdre G. Millington; Panther Books, 1965).

straight flight path for four minutes, a long time in terms of vulnerability to enemy interception. Yet despite the obvious dangers no aircraft were lost and 9,500 prints were produced. From these missions, new low-level obliques of the proposed glider landing and paratroop dropping zones in the invasion area were obtained, for study by the IXth Troop Carrier Command and the airborne divisions. In his book about the landings in Normandy by men of the 506th Regt, US 101st Airborne Division, called *Currahee! 'We Stand Alone'*[1], Donald Burgett writes that during the time they were at Honiton airfield waiting to go into combat, "the next few days were spent in briefing tents studying aerial photographs, maps and three-dimensional scale models of Normandy. Each paratrooper had to learn the whole operation by heart. ..." The photographs which helped them to do so were the products of these deliberate daylight reconnaissance missions. But the deception of a probable invasion much further east was still kept up, each mission in the planned invasion area being matched by two others, executed in exactly the same way, over the Pas de Calais. "For every reconnaissance sent to Western Normandy it was ruled that three should be sent somewhere, anywhere else," Lt-Gen Sir Frederick Morgan (COSSAC) noted in his book *Overture to Overlord*[2].

A Wurzburg defence radar installation on the French coast under attack by rocket-firing RAF Typhoons on D-day, June 6, 1944

[1]Hutchinson, 1967.
[2]Hodder & Stoughton, 1950.

Very low level Allied reconnaissance photograph of Germans (who can be seen scuttling for safety) erecting beach defences along the Normandy coast.

When weather or cloud conditions precluded photography by high-level reconnaissance aircraft accompanying the medium bombers, and when reports of visual observations were urgently required, these were relayed by pilots over the RT to the sector controller, who transmitted them to the reconnaissance centre at Advanced Headquarters. Thus such information could be made available within half an hour of a bombing attack. When photography by accompanying reconnaissance aircraft was possible, damage assessment pictures were taken at the same time.

In all, some 400 tactical reconnaissance sorties were flown by the US 9th Air Force during this period, plus 140 weather reconnaissance sorties. Throughout this time (May 15—June 6) maximum use was made of PR to provide the photographic coverage required by both the armies and the air forces. This effort was closely co-ordinated with the RAF and British units concerned, to make maximum use of available PR facilities. By the spring of 1944 (notes Andrew J. Brookes in his *Photo Reconnaissance–The Operational History*[1]) both 106 Wing and the 2 TAF PR squadrons were heavily committed to D-day preparations. Low level photography was particularly important, and the latest PR G-type, the Spitfire PR XIII, was often to be seen photographing the French coast obliquely from three to four miles off-shore so that landing-craft coxswains would have an idea of what they would see on D-day, followed by runs 1,500 yards from the beaches so that platoon commanders would be able to orientate themselves on the day".

[1] Ian Allan, 1975.

A Headquarters 9th Air Force Reconnaissance Report for the May 15—June 5 period lists the following nine tasks completed by the 9th Air Force Photographic Group, and shows the intensity of PR coverage before the Normandy landings:-
(1) Mosaic of the area within a 12-miles radius of the Liège bridges for a IXth Bomber Command study of the flak defences in the area prior to bombing operations.
(2) Coverage of all Luftwaffe-occupied airfields, and those previously occupied by the Luftwaffe (a highly mobile force, whose units could be rapidly re-deployed according to the tactical or defence situation) in northern France.
(3) Run-in strips for use in briefing IXth Troop Carrier Command pilots to assist them in making correct landfalls. [As will be emphasised later, these C-47/C-53 pilots, and the Dakota pilots of the RAF 46 Group, who were to drop the paratroops during the night preceding D-day, would in the majority of cases be making their first-ever flight over enemy territory—whereas most of the fighter, bomber and reconnaissance pilots had been over it many, many times before].
(4) Mosaics of the landing zones for gliders [whose pilots, too, would be over the hostile terrain for the first time] and of paratroop dropping zones, for the IXth Troop Carrier Command and the airborne divisions.
(5) Medium-scale coverage of all main roads in the invasion area, made every four days from May 23 until D-day.
(6) Medium-scale coverage of all bridges over the Loire, from Nantes to Orleans.
(7) Medium-scale coverage of all bridges over the Seine, as far inland as Paris.
(8) On D-day-minus 1, special large-scale coverage of the landing and dropping zones, to enable IXth Troop Carrier Command and the airborne divisions to study obstacles reported to be under construction in those areas. [German defences against airborne landings, as well as those against landings from the sea, were both ingenious and terrible—for example, the anti-glider poles known as "Rommel's asparagus"].
(9) Eleven special sorties flown to obtain low-level oblique pictures of under-water beach defences, aircraft photographing their targets at zero feet and producing invaluable information on the obstacles, also disclosing the Teller mines[1] and high-explosive shells fastened to many of them. This reconnaissance information assisted the Royal Navy in dealing with underwater hazards.

Reports from fighter-bomber pilots and crews of medium bombers supplemented such deliberate reconnaissance operations, since emphasis was placed in training on accurate observation and reporting, eye-witness information often bringing striking results.

Thus on April 23, 1944, fighter-bomber pilots returning from a mission over the Namur marshalling yards reported the largest concentration of rolling-stock they had ever seen. This information was received at Advanced Headquarters, 9th Air Force, at 1440hr that day. By 1944hr a fighter-bomber group and four groups of medium bombers had attacked this target, causing heavy damage to points, sidings and rolling-stock.

The two largest groups (Nos 83 and 84) in the 2nd Tactical Air Force, which was the Commonwealth, European and RAF component of the Allied Expeditionary Air Force, made their own vivid and intense contribution to the pre-*Overlord* operations. These were groups equipped entirely with fighter aircraft, armed with cannons, rockets and bombs and inflicting great physical and morale damage upon the Germany Army and

[1]So called because they were plate-shaped, these were the largest German anti-tank mines, armed with a 12lb explosive charge.

112

Air Force personnel whose installations and equipment they attacked. While No 84 Group was European in character with RAF, Czech, French, Polish, Belgian and Norwegian pilots, more than half of the strength of No 83 was made up of RCAF squadrons. Both the groups have had their histories written, and the style of these is so economical and modest that it conveys in an extraordinary way the energetic gallantry of the airmen preparing the way for the soldiers who were to enter (or re-enter, in the case of the British Army) the continent of Europe. Thus the genesis and the aggressive spirit of No 83 Group were concisely described by the chronicler:-

"From the time it was formed until D-day (he writes)[1], the Group was concerned with training, and periodical operations against enemy defences in north-west Europe. The training consisted of developing the organisation of a tactical air force and in practising the technique required for this type of aerial warfare.

"Of special note in this connection was Exercise *Limbo,* carried out in October 1943, the object of which was to practise the movement, deployment and working of the First Canadian Army Headquarters in conjunction with No 83 Group Headquarters in the field. The technique of running the main battle room, army operations room, intelligence centres (Army and RAF) and the RAF operations room was tried out as realistically as possible".

Here were the beginnings of that Army/Air Force co-operation, inaugurated so successfully in the Mediterranean theatre in 1942/43, which was to carry No 83 Group through to Luneburg in Germany—and other elements of the Allied Tactical Air Forces to similar victorious destinations in 1945. The group's historian continues:-

"Operations against the enemy developed slowly at first, increasing in tempo as more crews and aircraft became available. The main tasks were fighter sweeps against enemy defences, and reconnaissance. Up to August 31, 1943, No 83 Group destroyed 24 enemy aircraft, probably destroyed 3 and damaged 23; 5,445 sorties were flown, 199 tons of bombs were dropped and 35 pilots were lost. However, September 1943 alone saw 4,777 sorties, destroying 14 enemy aircraft, probably destroying 2 and damaging 15. In October and November 1943 the process continued and large numbers of fighter sweeps were carried out over Occupied France, with considerable success. In November particularly there were a number of concentrated attacks on special constructional works in the Pas de Calais and Cherboug areas[2]. In all, during this month, there were 2,672 operational sorties, destroying 12 enemy aircraft for the loss of 18 pilots and 21 aircraft.[3] 126 tons of bombs were dropped by Typhoon bombers. Weather was always a limiting factor during this period, but the attacks were maintained whenever possible. On the 20th December 1943 there was a particularly successful operation carried out by No 421 Sqn (Spitfire IXs) which was on a fighter sweep over France, called under the code name *Ramrod 375,* in which seven enemy fighters were destroyed and three others damaged. ...

"On January 21, 1944, No 83 Group destroyed its 100th German aircraft.

"In the three months from February to June 1944 the Group, together with all air forces of the Allies based in Britain, operated in great strength preparing the way for the

---

[1] *A Short Historical Account of No 83 Group during the period 1st April, 1943, to the end of the war in Europe,* Compiled and written by Sqn Ldr D. R. Morgan, BA.
[2] Part of Operation *Crossbow* against the V-1 launching sites.
[3] This almost casual statistic shows that air supremacy was not acquired by the Allies without considerable cost, and that even in late 1943 the Luftwaffe was still a force to be reckoned with.

landings, by softening-up the enemy's ability to resist. Operational control of all No 83 Group squadrons was vested in a Combined Control Centre at Uxbridge, to enable Group Headquarters and its associated units to be free to plan and move to the Continent. ..."

The other Group in the 2nd Allied Tactical Air Force armed with fighters and fighter-bombers for offensive operations was No 84, which began to form in June 1943 at Cowley Barracks, Oxford, headquarters of the British 2nd Army. During the following months several exercises were held (code-named *Punch, Judy, Columbine,* etc) until November of that pre-*Overlord* year; but during the 1943-44 winter the group became associated with the 1st Canadian instead of the 2nd British Army, and gradually its wing strength was built up. No 84's historian[1] commented:-

"The squadrons, however, were not operationally under the control of 84 Group but worked under the Air Defence of Great Britain. At this time also, men who had seen the RAF and the Army in joint action with the Royal Navy in the Mediterranean theatre came to strengthen the group with their experience of actual operations, and Air Marshal Sir Arthur Coningham, KCB, DSO, MC, DFC, AFC, in a brilliant speech to the whole of the staff, outlined the war situation as he saw it, likely developments, and the part the group would be called upon to play. ..."

This is a most important point, for "Mary" (i.e. "Maori") Coningham had been an outstanding commander of the Desert Air Force. One of the interesting facets of Operation *Overlord* is the number of leaders who had made their military reputations in the Mediterranean theatre and came to take over the chief posts for this last great campaign against Nazi Germany—Eisenhower himself, Tedder, Montgomery, Doolittle and Coningham. The Germans also transferred some of their leaders from the Mediterranean theatre, for example, Rommel and Peltz.

The chronicler of No 84 Group went on to describe the prime purpose of its operations during the early months of 1944, and to underline the seriousness of the new German threat which they were countering:-

"Operations during this period—or at least from January onwards—were directed mainly against what were called *No Ball* targets, that is, flying-bomb installations. The sites, discovered and photographed by, amongst others, 35 Wing,[2] were found to be ranged, in various stages of completion, all along the French coast from Pas de Calais to the Cherbourg Peninsula.[3] There could be no doubt of the menace they represented, nor of the constant attacks that must be made against them. One site, it is known, was completed and destroyed no fewer than nine times. Later in the period, the sites were much simplified and much more difficult to locate; one operation by Typhoons was to drop bombs to blow away the camouflage so that the recce Mustang flying with the formation could take photographs.

"When in June 1944 flying bombs began to be fired at the United Kingdom, Anti-Diver patrols, as they were called, became a complementary operation to the destruction of the firing sites.

"With the approach of summer, the Group squadrons, still operationally under

[1]J. Robinson.
[2]This Mustang and Spitfire reconnaissance wing was part of No 84 Group.
[3]The attacks from both weapons (VIs and V2s) were aimed principally at London, with a secondary group of targets in the south.

ADGB[1], took part in escorting and covering the general destruction by bombers of enemy communications, marshalling yards, bridges etc from Belgium to Brittany, adding their own quota wherever possible. On May 21, for example, following the release for attack of trains in hostile and enemy-occupied territories[2], a terrific onslaught was made by between 1,200 and 1,300 aircraft of 2nd TAF and the 8th and 9th USAAF. At least 129 locos were destroyed and 156 damaged.

"Meanwhile, also, the Group shared in the attacks on enemy airfields which forced the German Air Force away from the coastal areas back to such places as Evreux. The consequence was that during the Normandy landings, the GAF was at an inconvenient distance from the bridgehead, and had to attempt hurried, but ineffective, exploitation of strips in the Flers and Argentan area.

"With the approach of D-day it became necessary—in fact vital—to destroy the radar installations which gave complete cover to the whole of the Western European seaboard, making it impossible for aircraft or shipping to approach the Continent without being detected at a greater or lesser distance according to the height of the approaching machine. 84 Group aircraft attacked, among others, the following installations: Cap d'Antifer, Dieppe, Boulogne, Cap Gris Nez, Caen-Douvres, Berck, Abbeville, Fécamp, St Valery en Caux, Fruges-Predefin, Le Havre, Cap de la Hague."

This is a remarkable list, showing how strongly and comprehensively the Germans had organised their defensive radar cover along the Channel coast during the four years since their armies had reached Dunkirk. Even more remarkable, though, in a different way, are the next few paragraphs in the 84 Group history, describing an attack on a *Wurzburg*[3] radar station and relating a German eye-witness account of it. These show with what daring and resolution the attacks on such targets were pressed home by the fighter-bomber pilots. The group's historian says:-

"A good example of the hazards of this type of operation was an attack on May 24 on a radar aircraft reporting station at Cap de la Hague/Joburg. The target—a hoarding, a *Giant Wurzburg* and huts—was on the northern end of the Cherbourg Peninsula, always a heavily defended area. The enemy, aware that his radar installations were being systematically removed, had in fact even strengthened the anti-aircraft defences covering such targets. The attacks, originally planned for 0650hr take-off but delayed by thick fog until 1007hr, was made by four aircraft of 198 Sqn and four aircraft of 609 Sqn, all Typhoons. Sqn Ldr Niblett of 198 Sqn (killed on June 2 when attacking a similar target at Dieppe) led the mission.

"The attack was made at zero feet and the pilots' report reads:-

'40x60lb R/P and cannon fired. Numerous strikes on hoarding. One of missing aircraft seen to crash at base of hoarding. Two concrete pillboxes strafed with unobserved results. F/Sgt Vallely and Fg Off Freeman collided on the run-in. F/Sgt Vallely crashed in flames over the target. Fg Off Freeman seen crashing in vicinity of target'."

What makes this report even more vivid is the description of the attack given some months later by a German PoW, who had witnessed it and described it thus to his interrogator:-

[1] Air Defence of Great Britain.
[2] I.e., under the Transportation Plan.
[3] One of the earliest types of German radar, originally with a range of 25 miles.

"Three Typhoons came in from the valley flying very low. The second aircraft got a direct hit from 37mm flak which practically shot off its tail. The pilot, however, managed to keep some sort of control and continued straight at the target. He dived below the level of the target structure, fired rockets into it, and then tried at the last moment to clear. The third aircraft, in trying to avoid the damaged Typhoon, touched the latter's fuselage with a wing tip. Both aircraft locked together and crashed some 100yds beyond. The radar installation was never again serviceable. Of the cables leading up to the target, 23 out of 28 major leads were severed."

Pre-*Overlord* operations by the American light and medium bombers—A-20s, B-25s and B-26s of the 9th Air Force—have already been referred to: their British opposite numbers were the RAF Mosquitos, Bostons and Mitchells of No 2 Group in the 2nd Tactical Air Force. This group had formerly been in RAF Bomber Command; then on June 1, 1943 it came under the control of Fighter Command, and on the same date the Tactical Air Force was inaugurated within the Command. No 2 Group itself was commanded from May 27, 1943, by one of the most forceful leaders of the RAF during the Second World War, Air Vice-Marshal B. E. Embry.

Early in April 1944 an exercise called *Smash II* was held in which 12 aircraft of No 226 Sqn (Mitchell IIs) took part: its aim was to practise and develop the fire support for an assault on a defended coast, in co-operation with the Army and the Navy. Within two months this was to be done "for real"; meanwhile, No 2 Group kept up its almost daily pre-invasion attacks on enemy defences.

The group was equipped, at the time of its operations in support of *Overlord,* with three types of light/medium bombers—Bostons, Mitchells and Mosquitos. In addition to its RAF, RAAF and RNZAF aircrew it had Dutch, French and Polish squadrons. Previously, it had had three Ventura and three Boston squadrons, but the Venturas were withdrawn from service and those squadrons re-armed with Mosquito VIs, and the number of Boston squadrons was reduced to two; so the real hitting power of No 2 Group in the pre-Normandy landings period lay in its four Mitchell and six Mosquito squadrons.

B-25 Mitchells were also used by the US 9th Air Force, which provided the other tactical bomber component of the Allied Tactical Air Force and additionally had A-20s (Bostons) and B-26s (Marauders). The presence of so many light and medium bombers over Europe in 1943/44 marked a change in the character of the air war in the West. After the early failures of the RAF Blenheims and Battles in 1939/40 this type of aircraft, operating in daylight, had been virtually banished from the skies; operations over Europe had been performed by fighters and heavy bombers, by RAF Fighter Command in day sweeps over Occupied France and by RAF Bomber Command over Germany by night; then also, from 1942, by the USAAF heavy bombers in daylight. The presence of so many tactical day bombers from 1943 onwards, and the part they played in the Operation *Overlord* air operations, derived from two factors: gradual Allied control of the air by day, which allowed the light/medium bombers to go out in increasing strength; and the American aircraft which were used for these operations—the A-20s, B-25s (Mitchells) and B-26s. Britain produced nothing like these aircraft, or the American Baltimores which were used by the RAF in the Middle East, during the war; her production concentrated largely upon heavy bombers and fighters. The role which these

US types played in Europe, attacking enemy installations, was an important one in the "softening up" offensive before the Normandy landings. The Mosquito fighter-bombers were the British teeth of No 2 Group: their bombs and gunfire at low level were devastating weaponry, and their speed gave them greater invulnerability than that of the Bostons, Marauders and Mitchells. Much has already been written about the uniqueness and versatility of the Mosquito, and its successful use in so many spheres of action made it one of the outstanding aircraft of the Second World War.

No 2 Group was one of the most effective users of the type, and its commander from May 27, 1943, has given a vivid picture of its operations. In his autobiographical book *Mission Completed*[1], Air Chief Marshal Sir Basil Embry (as he became) writes about one of its first major tasks, destruction of sites for launching rockets and pilotless bombs against London. After saying that on October 3, 1943, the Mosquito and Boston squadrons "carried out an interesting operation" against a number of transformer stations between Paris and Nantes—"the first of a large number of low attacks made by the Group after being transferred to the 2nd TAF"—he writes thus of operations against the *Ski* (launching) sites:-

"The Group opened its offensive against these targets on 5th November in conjunction with other forces, and also on the centres of the Todt organisation, which was charged with the work of building the launching sites. One of our first targets was the village of Audinghen, said to be the headquarters of the Todt organisation. We attacked several times from medium altitude with our Boston and Mitchell squadrons, and by the 25th November there was literally nothing left to bomb.

"Our early attacks on the launching sites from medium altitude showed that although we were able to place our bombs accurately in the target area, it was no easy matter to score a direct hit on a vital part of the site. Photographs of early attacks showed bomb craters right across the site but no damage to the three buildings or the launching platform. This was worrying, because not only did it mean that it would take a long time to destroy the hundred-odd sites now nearing completion, but to have to return several times to the same target always caused higher casualties, as was again proved to us early in this offensive. In one of our first attacks in the Pas de Calais area we used 46 aircraft without loss, but 14 were damaged by flak[2]. Three days later we attacked the same place with 48 aircraft, and had one shot down and 27 damaged. This was a fair indication of the rapidity with which the Germans strengthened their anti-aircraft defences round a target they thought we were intent on destroying.

"It was obvious that if these sites were to be put out of action, really accurate pinpoint bombing would have to be done, and so I decided to try out our Mosquitos at low altitude against them. To assess the problems of operating Mosquitos against the sites, I took part in two early attacks. We used 18 Mosquitos, flying in three echelons of six aircraft each, and selected the three buildings on the site as our aiming points. We flew across the Channel at 50 feet, made an accurate landfall and found the target without difficulty. Taking the enemy completely by surprise, I can recall no damage from flak. We hit two of

[1]Methuen & Co, 1957.

[2]"What do you mean by 'Flak', Embry?" the author records being asked by a senior officer. "When I explained that it was the German term for anti-aircraft artillery, he said, "Oh! 'Archie'- this is what we called it in the last war. You don't want to bother about that, we always flew through it!" I laughed, "Well, have a go in this war, sir, because it might help promotion!".

"Literally nothing left to bomb": all that was left of a V-weapon launching site after attacks by Allied bombers

the buildings and though the photographic interpreters assessed them as only slightly damaged and not destroyed, still, the results were encouraging.

* * *

"Between November 1943, when we began operating against these sites, and mid-May 1944, when the Group was switched to attack targets associated with operation *Overlord,* we flew 4,710 sorties against *No Ball* targets, which was the code name given to rocket and flying-bomb sites and their storage and manufacturing centres. In all these sorties we did not a lose a single aircraft to enemy fighters, but had 41 shot down and 419 damaged by fire from the ground. Considering how strongly defended many of these targets were by light and heavy flak, and that about a fifth of the missions were flown at minimum height, it was a remarkable record, and it was due in no small measure to the meticulous attention the Group operations planning staff paid to routeing our formations, to the work of our anti-flak section [which Embry had set up within the No 2 Group operational planning staff] and to the careful allocation of targets, depending on their anti-aircraft defences, to the medium- or low-altitude attack squadrons.

"During the period the Group was employed in the assault on the flying-bomb sites, a total of 103 were attacked by the combined forces of British Bomber Command, the British 2nd TAF and the United States 8th and 9th Air Forces, with in all 93 damaged beyond repair. Of these No 2 Group was responsible for destroying 32. The following table, which shows the results by commands and types of aircraft together with the average bomb tonnage expended to destroy a site, and the casualties to our aircraft per site destroyed, is interesting:

"Command	Aircraft	Number of sites destroyed	Average bomb tonnage per site	Aircraft casualties per sites destroyed
US 8th AF	Fortress	30	195.1	1.1
US 9th AF	Marauder	26	223.5	0.89
No 2 Group, British Tactical AF	Mitchell Boston Mosquito VI	11½ 1½ 19	224.8 344.3 39.8	0.95 2.0 0.87
Nos 83 and 84 Groups 2nd TAF	Typhoon fighter-bomber	5	266.8	0.68"

In May 1944, the month when No 2 Group, in the words of its Air Officer Commanding, was "switched to attack targets associated with *Overlord",* the group continued its *Flower* operations (that is, attacks on airfields), which had been going on since early in April and were undertaken by night as well as by day ("I was anxious", said Embry of the early weeks of his command, "that the Group should be trained for night

RAF 2nd Tactical Air Force Mitchells of No 226 Sqn, based at Hartford Bridge, Hampshire, bomb targets in Normandy

operations"). It attacked railway centres, depots and marshalling yards. Other targets were field batteries, gun positions and coastal defences; navigational beam stations; bridges; vehicles on roads; and—at intervals—*No Ball* targets, the rocket and flying-bomb sites that had been attacked so intensively since November 1943. On February 18 the Group had made its spectacular raid on Amiens prison, 18 Mosquitos being employed on an operation to burst open its walls to release members of the French Resistance incarcerated there, in an operation dramatically code-named *Jericho;*[1] then on April 11 a similarly brilliant sortie was made against a building in The Hague where the Gestapo kept records of members of the Dutch resistance movement, and it was completely destroyed. In addition, during the two months preceding D-day, aircraft of No 2 Group made many *Ranger* patrols when they picked-off small targets like staff cars, store dumps, buildings and vehicles with cannon and machine-gun fire, when no suitable targets for bombing were seen. Early in his command of the Group, Embry had decided

[1]See *The Gates Burst Open,* by Col Livry-Level (tr by Pamela Search), Aries Publishers, 1955; and *And the Walls came tumbling down,* by Jack Fishman, Souvenir Press, 1982, for differing accounts of this raid.

that it should be "able to find and hit any target down to a single building". He considered that its targets should "as far as possible be isolated factories, power stations, bridges, headquarters or indeed any small target within our power to destroy". But once *Overlord* was launched, he "anticipated that the kind of objective we would be required to attack would be fuel and ammunition dumps, bridges, radar stations, heavy gun positions and headquarters"—and all such kinds of targets figure in the Group's Operations Record Books for the weeks prior to the Allied landings in Normandy. In his *Mission Completed,* Embry refers bluntly to pre-*Overlord* operations by the air forces as "the vast scheme of demolition which was part of the pre-invasion plan", and of June 6, 1944, he says:-

"On the morning of D-day itself, our Mitchell squadrons attacked with great accuracy gun positions directly threatening the approach of the great armada to the Normandy beach-head, and our Bostons flying at sea level laid the smoke screen over the invasion craft.

"From now on the task of the Group was to work more closely in unison with the armies which the air forces had helped to land. ..."

While the USAAF 9th Air Force and the RAF 2nd Tactical Air Force with their medium/light bombers, fighters, fighter-bombers and reconnaissance aircraft had been destroying German army capability within range of the invasion beaches, and had photographed every yard of terrain near where the landings were to be made, a highly specialised Group in RAF Bomber Command, No 100 Group, had been contributing to the attrition of Luftwaffe strength by counter-measure operations.

Its formation in November 1943, and the various types of aircraft and equipment it used, have already been briefly referred to (pages 17 and 18). In the context of *Overlord,* the group's most immediately applicable contribution to the Allied landings—in addition to fighter support, by *Serrate*-equipped and intruder squadrons—was the provision of a great anti-radar screen to hide the armada of ships crossing the Channel from the German early-warning system. This was an Anglo-American success, in that the equipment used—*Mandrel,* which jammed the German radar—was British-developed and the aircraft in which it was put were American—Boeing B-17G Flying Fortresses, which had the space and power for it and could operate at 28-30,000ft. In a similar alliance of equipment and aircraft, Fortresses of the USAAF 803rd Sqn carried RAF jamming equipment on the night of June 5/6, 1944, to conceal the landings of American forces from the German long-range warning stations, operating with Nos 199 and 214 Squadrons. These successes in confusing enemy radar as to Allied intentions resulted from the development of equipment, fitting it into aircraft and training crews in its use, achieved in less than seven months before D-day.

Had some watcher in the skies been able to observe activities above the English Channel prior to the landings in Normandy, he would have seen not only the fighter-bombers, medium and heavy bombers and fighters of the Allied air forces but also the counter-measures aircraft jamming German defence radars. For not only was a *Mandrel* screen thrown over the invasion fleet; the RAF created two 'spoof' armadas heading for the coast of France, simulated a bomber stream flying over the River Somme area, and a mock 'invasion' in the Caen and Cap d'Antifer areas.

Two squadrons, one of Lancasters (the famous 617 of the dams raid) and one of Stirlings (218), flew steady courses back and forth for hours over two fleets of small boats which put out from Newhaven. Towed above these boats were balloons with radar reflectors in them which would produce, on the enemy operator's screen, the impression of a 10,000-ton ship. No 617's fleet headed for Cap d'Antifer (Operation *Taxable*) while No 218's made towards Boulogne (Operation *Glimmer*), while above them the bomber crews dropped out bundle after bundle of *Window,* these aluminium strips giving a radar picture of ships. Strikingly, it is recorded that at the end of their night's operation, when the sky began to lighten from the east, the bomber crews could see below them some of the transport and glider fleets heading for Normandy.

These squadrons were not part of No 100 Group; the only counter-measure equipment they carried was *Window.* Likewise the mock 'invasion' (code-named *Titanic*) was not one of the group's operations, though two of the four squadrons involved—Nos 90, 138, 149 and 161—had a 'special duties' role (Nos 138 and 161). The 'ghost' bomber stream along the River Somme, however, was partly a No 100 Group operation in that one of the two squadrons involved was No 214, which had been equipped with B-17G Flying Fortresses loaned by the USAAF. Five of its aircraft, with four Lancasters of No 101 Sqn, created the illusion of a bomber stream by dropping *Window* and using *Airborne Cigar,* the transmitter which jammed German radars. Supporting them in this were the ground-based jamming transmitters in the south of England, which blotted out the frequencies used by the Luftwaffe night fighters, thus protecting the Allied transport force flying to Normandy.

During the landings a large number of No 100 Group Mosquitos were sent out on patrols, encountering very little enemy fighter opposition. One conclusion drawn from an analysis of the figures for the number of enemy aircraft attacked during May and June 1944 was that there were fewer Messerschmitt Me110s in the area. An indication of how these No 100 Group squadrons operated in their joint roles, intruding to destroy enemy fighters and affording airborne counter-measure protection to the RAF bomber force, is given by the group's summary of operations for June 1944:-

"During June the intercepted traffic has indicated that the enemy is making increasing use of assembly beacons. In the latter part of the month, a number of *Serrate* patrols have been sent to the favourite beacons, with a considerable measure of success. This, and an escort of the bomber screen, now appear as the most profitable types of patrol. The results of the last week in June, when only these two types of patrol were carried out, are encouraging, for seven enemy aircraft were destroyed from 74 sorties despatched.

"During the month the intruder squadrons—namely Nos 515, 85 and 157—shot down 15 enemy aircraft and damaged five more. Towards the end of the month Nos 85 and 157 were employed on anti-flying bomb patrols and destroyed nine. ...

"No 192 Sqn carried out 134 successful investigational patrols. Nos 803[1] and 199 were employed throughout the period on *Mandrel* screen operations; 107 sorties were flown and one Stirling is missing. *ABC* and *Jostle* jamming in support of Bomber Command was carried out by No 214 Sqn (which for this role was equipped with B-17 Flying Fortresses). One Fortress is missing, and one Me410 was destroyed, as a result of the 25 sorties made".

[1]The USAAF B-17/24 squadron.

These No 100 Group operations demonstrated the scientific application of radio and radar to the air-to-air battle. Their application to the air-to-sea battle of aircraft against submarines and surface craft was demonstrated by RAF Coastal Command, whose task in the pre-*Overlord* period was the protection of Allied shipping and the supplies it carried. In particular, the role of the Command was to guard from U-boat attack the massive Allied armada which would cross the English Channel on D-day to land and supply the armies entering France; these U-boats would come chiefly from ports in the Bay of Biscay.

By the end of March there were signs that the German Navy was reducing the number of U-boats in the Atlantic, presumably to concentrate them for possible counter-invasion operations. Coastal Command confirmed this trend during April and May; there was a lull in U-boat operations in the Atlantic, but concurrently a build-up of U-boats in the Bay of Biscay ports. This lull, said the AOC-in-C Coastal Command (Air Chief Marshal Sir Sholto Douglas) in a despatch he wrote for the Air Ministry after *Overlord,* "permitted an intensive training programme for the Leigh-light squadrons in the United Kingdom. ... The urgent need for Leigh-light aircraft over the past two years had meant that aircrews turned over to this role had had insufficient time to devote to training, and the standard of homing and Leigh-light manipulation was not as high as it might have been. Ten weeks' intensive training was carried out by the UK-based Liberator and Wellington searchlight squadrons, and when D-day came the standard was much improved". The Leigh-light, named after its inventor Sqn Ldr H. de V. Leigh, was an airborne searchlight lowered beneath the aircraft. Introduced in mid-1942, it enabled night attacks to be made on surfaced U-boats.

In summing-up the operational policy which had to be adopted by Coastal Command before *Overlord* the AOC-in-C said in his despatch: "On the assumption that the enemy would direct his U-boat offensive principally against our invasion convoys, the Admiralty [with whom the RAF maritime arm worked in close concert] appreciated that the bulk of his U-boats would operate from the Bay ports and endeavour to penetrate the south-west approaches to the Bristol, St George's and English Channels. ... The main focus of our anti-U-boat operations was therefore to be in the SW approaches and the effort directed to protecting Atlantic convoys would be drastically reduced. It was also necessary to provide to some extent against the passage of U-boats through the northern transit area and also against the possibility of the movement of U-boats through the North Sea. These areas had however to be regarded as of secondary importance when compared with the SW approaches. ..."

Coastal Command had four Groups, and of these No 19 Group at Plymouth had the most onerous tasks in early 1944, for these were: to provide adequate air cover in the south-west approaches and to protect the flanks of the Allied invasion convoys; to provide cover or close escort to Allied invasion convoys in the SW approaches; and to hunt and destroy enemy U-boats attempting to attack Allied invasion convoys in the SW approaches. The group was reinforced for its crucial role of protecting the cross-Channel convoys to a strength of 25 squadrons, about 350 aircraft—Sunderlands, Wellingtons, Liberators, Mosquitos, Halifaxes, Beaufighters and Swordfish.

How No 19 Group set about protecting the convoys from the U-boat has been well described in Alfred Price's book *Aircraft versus Submarine:*[1] "A stretch of water some

[1]William Kimber, 1973.

20,000 square miles in extent, enclosing the north-west coast of France and the southern coast of Ireland and running eastwards along the English Channel to the Cherbourg peninsula, was to be intensivly patrolled by day and by night, so that a U-boat on the surface anywhere in that area would be seen on radar at least once every thirty minutes."

The crucial phrase here is "a U-boat on the surface", that is, one that was re-charging its batteries or topping-up its supply of compressed air; but if a U-boat was fitted with a schnorkel breathing device it could remain submerged for very much longer periods: "as Allied Intelligence officers knew [writes Price], this was scheduled to be fitted to all operational German U-boats. But, in spite of the most strenuous efforts on the part of the dockyard personnel, the programme had slipped badly. For example, by the beginning of June 1944 only nine of the forty-nine U-boats of the *Landwirt Group,* allocated to the counter-invasion task, carried this modification: many of the conversion kits were to remain, unused, in their packing cases, trapped in goods yards by the systematic Allied aerial bombardment of the French railway system. ..."

The way in which No 19 Group kept surveillance over the vast area of water through which the U-boats would come on their way up from the Bay of Biscay was by what became known as "Cork" patrols, rectangular areas of different sizes according to the varied ranges of the aircraft patrolling them. The aircraft flew along the invisible sides of these rectangles, sweeping the seas with their radar. The area they covered "blocked-off" the south-west approaches from the south coast of Ireland to the west coast of Brittany; hence the patrols were known as "Cork" because in effect they "bottled-up" the English Channel by day and by night. Some of the patrols involved Coastal Command aircraft flying so near to the coast of German-occupied France that Allied fighters were kept in readiness to protect them.

Apart from the RAF accounts of individual successes against U-boats by Sunderland, Liberator and Wellington crews, the best evidence of the effectiveness of the 19 Group defensive screen comes from the German naval officer whose task it was to destroy any Allied vessel taking part in the landings before it reached the Normandy shore: Admiral Theodor Krancke, commander, *Marinegruppenkommando West* (Naval Forces, West). During May, he wrote in his diary that his forces "were almost invariably attacked from the air as soon as they left harbour and suffered numerous hits ... darkness provided no relief. ... The operations of motor torpedo boats were handicapped by strong enemy patrols which prevented intended attacks and the laying of mines. ..."

During this period of intensive preparation for the Allied landings, and of protection for them like that provided by the anti-U-boat offensive, the question of France herself—the ally upon whose territory the Allied armies were soon to land—loomed ever larger in the minds of the planners of *Overlord.* In the preparatory attacks before D-day upon German forces and installations in Occupied France, upon the airfields, radar sites, gun positions, troop concentrations, railways, bridges and roads, French property and lives were inevitably being put at risk; yet it was important for the Allies that the French populace should be on the side of the liberation armies.

The French Resistance movement was made up of many elements, some associated with the UK-based SOE (Special Operations Executive) and some not; nor could the Free French forces outside France claim to speak with one voice, for while General de Gaulle provided a figurehead and leadership his influence and authority were not universally accepted, and the attitude of the Allied leaders towards him was ambivalent. However, from 1943 onwards a new element entered into French affairs with the growth of the Maquis movement, formed by young men who had taken to the woods and mountains rather than be forced to labour by and for the Germans. The numbers of these men, particularly in the mountainous south-eastern area of France, had grown sufficiently for the Germans and the Vichy authorities to have to use 10,000 troops in a concentrated drive upon them during early 1944. They were therefore a formidable factor in the French Resistance; and although the risks involved in supplying them by air were great, and the practical results of such operations were hard to assess, the decision was made to drop containers. In addition the other parts of the French Resistance movement, those who were not guerrillas like the Maquis (whose forces numbered about 100,000 by the late spring of 1944 and had taken over large areas of territory) but operated within the SOE organisation, also received a substantial increase in supplies—all delivered by air—from the UK. The figures for the number of sorties made by British and US bombers to drop supplies into France tell their own tale against the background of *Overlord* preparations. For while in the third quarter of 1943 there were 327 sorties and in the fourth quarter 101 (all British), in the first quarter of 1944 there were 609 (557 British and 52 American) and in the second quarter—April, May and June—there were 1,269 (748 British and 521 American). In the April-June 1944 period, RAF aircraft delivered 1,162 tons of supplies and USAAF aircraft 524 tons. The author of *Grand Strategy,* Vol V of the *History of the Second World War*[1], John Ehrman, comments that this was "a substantial effort at the peak of the air campaign, it came at the right time, and it did more than anything else to prepare its recipients, morally as well as materially, for what lay ahead. ..."

This increase in supplies to the French Resistance during the build-up period of *Overlord* implied a greater number of aircraft being involved, as was indeed the case, particularly with participation by RAF Bomber Command squadrons from the autumn of 1943. Supplies arrived over France from the north and from the south, from the UK and from North Africa; they were dropped by the Royal Air Force and by the US Army Air Forces. The historian of the SOE, M. R. D. Foot, in his *SOE in France*[2] volume in the official *History of the Second World War,* describes well the growing crescendo of support from the skies to the French resisters; how, with some reluctantly-given assistance by RAF Bomber Command, the numbers grew from the original two Special Duties squadrons (Nos 138 and 161) operating from "the carefully camouflaged special duties airfield at Tempsford, west of Cambridge":

"By an informal arrangement 138 Sqn concentrated on dropping operations by SOE; while 161 handled the comparatively few other clandestine drops and all landing operations[3], dropping for SOE when it had aircraft to spare. Both squadrons took part also from time to time in ordinary bomber raids, or in other tasks that required their special navigational skills. In return, in the autumn of 1943 they were joined occasionally at Tempsford by Stirling squadrons of Bomber Command, seconded from bombing to special duty operations; Harris was ready to part for a time with his least effective four-

[1] HMSO, 1956.
[2] HMSO, 1966
[3] For first-hand accounts of these see *Black Lysander,* by John Nesbitt-Dufort (Jarrolds, 1973) and *We Landed by Moonlight,* by Hugh Verity (Ian Allan, 1978); also *Wings of the Night The Secret Missions of Group Captain Pickard,* by Alexander Hamilton (William Kimber, 1977).

engined aircraft, less effective even than the Halifax as a bomber. Lancasters were unavailable for SOE[1]. At the end of the year two American special duty squadrons with Liberators and Dakotas came to stay at Tempsford for a short final polishing-up of their techniques. These Americans moved early in 1944 to Alconbury, and later in the spring to Harrington, continuing their special work; and by a particular effort several score 3 Group and 38 (Transport) Group Stirlings and Albermarles and some 46 Group Dakotas were employed for supply dropping in February, March and April 1944. Meanwhile a few of 624 Squadron's Halifaxes, occasionally assisted by American Liberators, had been dropping agents and supplies into southern France from Blida near Algiers. Lastly, in the summer of 1944, while major operations were in progress in France, some mass drops of supplies were made to French Maquis by large formations of the 8th USAAF, flying B-17 Fortresses".

The USAAF supply-dropping operations from the UK were given the code name *Carpetbagger;* four squadrons (40 B-24s) were involved in this work by the end of May 1944. The first *Carpetbagger* missions were flown from Tempsford in early January 1944; the USAAF supply-dropping squadrons moved to Harrington in late March 1944, and in the three-month period March-May 1944 completed 213 out of 368 attempted sorties.

But whatever pressure the Allies put upon the Germans by the air, by strategic bombing, by destroying communications, by neutralising defences and by whittling-down the Luftwaffe, the German Army in the west was still undefeated; it had not fought a battle since its victorious march to the sea in 1940, and looked menacingly across the Channel from behind the defences which Field Marshal Rommel had been busy making even more formidable since the end of 1943. Allied aircraft had made sure of air superiority, but the Allied armies still had to go ashore, from the greatest armada of ships the world had ever seen, and fight their way up the defended beaches; and in advance of the seaborne assault went the airborne forces—soldiers pitched into battle from the air, by parachutes or gliders. These, to paraphrase Shakespeare, were the bravest soldiers of them all; for there were inherent risks in their means of reaching the battlefield, before they ever started to fight. The slow transport aircraft, or the gliders, were vulnerable to ground fire; if the parachute troops were dropped too low they didn't stand a chance, and the gliders were committed to a landing in the darkness once they had been released—they were unable to clear any obstacles which might loom up. A further fatalistic aspect of the airborne forces' role was that, for most of them (apart from the divisions which had gone into Sicily), Normandy represented a first taste of operations. Unlike the bomber and fighter aircrew, transport crews could not go again and again over enemy territory to gain battle experience. They trained, and trained and trained; they exercised their techniques against obstacles simulating those they would meet in Normandy. When June 4, 1944, came they were ready to go. After the 24hr postponement because of weather they were ready to go again—in their C-47s/-53s/Dakotas, their Horsas and Hamilcars and Wacos, to seize or destroy crucial objectives inland before the seaborne forces came ashore. What was to happen, in simple terms, was that the American airborne divisions, the 82nd and 101st, were to go down at the Western end of the Allied assault area and the British 6th Airborne Division at the

[1]The AOC-in-C Bomber Command, Air Chief Marshal Sir Arthur Harris, was unwilling to tolerate any diminution of his force, whether for SOE or anti-U-boat operations or other theatres of war; he believed that the destruction of Germany by bombing would win the war for the Allies.

Eastern end. Having achieved their objectives they would, it was hoped, link up with the 21st Army Group driving in from the sea. What could not be foreseen, or planned for, or rehearsed, were the imponderable factors which might affect these hazardous operations—cloud, failure of aircraft to find the right dropping-zone, release at too low a height, wind strength, obstacles on the ground (either natural or German-planted), and terrain which might be more water than land, into which a heavily loaded parachutist[1] might—and did—sink without hope of recovery.

The air force units which had trained with the airborne soldiers and were to carry or tow them over Normandy were Nos 38 and 46 Groups of the RAF and IXth Troop Carrier Command of the USAAF. No 38 Group had ten squadrons—four of Albermarles, four of Stirlings and two of Halifaxes—and No 46 Group, formed on January 17, 1944, to support it, had five squadrons of Dakotas. The IXth Troop Carrier Command had three wings, Nos 50, 52 and 53; 50 Troop Carrier Wing had four groups (Nos 439, 440, 441 and 442); 52 had five (Nos 61, 313, 314, 315 and 316) and 53 had five (Nos 434, 435, 436, 437 and 438). Thus there were 14 groups, each of which had four squadrons, giving a total of 56 squadrons. Aircraft were Douglas C-47 Skytrains and C-53 Skytroopers, basically the same type except that the former could be converted into a freighter; both were used for glider towing. As at May 1, 1944, the total aircraft strength of the USAAF IXth Troop Carrier Command was 1,167, plus more than 100 CG-4A Waco gliders, which would each carry 15 troops. The RAF No 38 and 46 Groups had a total of 362 aircraft plus 61 in reserve; at June 1, 1944, it had 406 aircraft ready for operations and 1,120 gliders, of which 70 were the big Hamilcars (68ft long with a wing span of 110ft) able to carry 40 troops or up to nearly 8 tons of freight, and the rest Horsas (67ft long with an 88ft wing span), carrying 29 troops or up to three tons of freight.

This great transport fleet was to drop three airborne divisions into Normandy—the US Army 82nd and 101st and the British Army 6th Airborne Division—a few hours prior to the landings on the beaches, that is, in the early hours of D-day. The American airborne forces were given priority in the airlift because they had the task of seizing the crucial exits from the Cotentin peninsula, on the western flank of the Allied assault from the sea. To deceive the enemy as to the location of these parachute and glider drops, RAF Stirlings were to drop *Window* (metal foil giving a radar picture) in an area well south of the actual location. The C-47/53 fleet with approximately 17,000 men aboard was to fly from west to east across the Cotentin peninsula. The 101st Division had the main offensive operations after landing—to capture the landward exits from *Utah* beach (the most westerly assault area), to destroy the bridges on the road leading into Carentan, and to protect the southern flank of the forces coming in from the seaborne assault. Activities of the 82nd Division in the first phase were of a more defensive character.

The RAF airlift of the 6th Airborne Division was to approach the French coast on a south-westerly heading, making landfall between two rivers, the Orne and the Dives, having flown out from England in three streams crossing the south coast over Worthing, Littlehampton and Bognor Regis and turning south-westwards in mid-Channel. Major objectives of these forces on the left (eastern) flank of the Allied landings were bridges over the Caen Canal and the River Orne, to be captured after glider landings as close as

[1] The equipment he carried weighed about 100lb: see *Six Armies in Normandy*, by John Keegan; Jonathan Cape, 1982.

Components of the airborne force – Horsas, jeeps and troops. Some problem appears to be occurring in the glider

Operation Tow-rope. This photograph gives a good idea of the size of the Airspeed Horsa (88ft wingspan and 67ft in length)

"They trained, and trained and trained . . .":-
A jeep being unloaded from a Horsa glider, which has the name 'Gibbon's Goofers' chalked on it

RAF Halifaxes and Hamilcar gliders: just one airfield of those used by the airborne forces prior to their departure for Normandy as the Allied vanguard on the night of June 5/6, 1944

possible to them, and the German battery at Merville, near which 11 gliders were to land while an attack on it by 100 Lancasters of Bomber Command was taking place; subsequently, three gliders were to "pancake" inside the battery defences, then with the aid of about 1,300 men of the 3rd Parachute Brigade this dangerous threat to the British landings on *Juno* and *Sword* beaches—eastern end of the Allied assault—would be removed.

Long-term parameters implicit in the gathering-together of such vast forces—their training, detailed planning of individual objectives, equipment and fuel, ammunition, and supplies of all kinds once beach-heads had been established by the five divisions being put ashore—such parameters, plus strategic and political considerations within the purview of the Combined Chiefs of Staff who had approved the plans for *Overlord,* determined the approximate date when the great assault would begin. Shorter-term parameters, like the state of the tides on the French coast and the period of the moon, determined the date more precisely, and June 5, 1944—when low water came soon after dawn, after a night with a full moon—was decided upon by the army, navy and air force commanders of the *Overlord* forces under the Supreme Commander, General Eisenhower. However, there was one more pervasive factor, the weather. In the first days of June this was bad, and although final preparations continued to be made, on the 4th it became clear that conditions on the 5th would not be suitable for the supporting air operations. The Supreme Commander therefore decided upon a 24-hour postponement, subject to a decision to be taken at 9.30 p.m. that evening. The Naval commander, Admiral Ramsay, said that if the operation did not begin on the 6th there would have to be more than one day's postponement because of the need for his ships to refuel. If, however, there was to be a longer postponement the operation could not take place within the period when conditions were judged to be suitable for it.

At the crucial meeting in the invasion headquarters at Portsmouth on the evening of June 4th, while the weather forecasters had given a hope of temporary improvement with clearing skies which would allow the air forces to operate during the night of the 5th and early morning of the 6th, the commanders were not unanimous in their views. "The airmen, Tedder and Leigh-Mallory (wrote Maj-Gen E. K. G. Sixsmith in his book *Eisenhower as Military Commander*)[1], were still doubtful and Montgomery still anxious to go. The decision was for Eisenhower himself and those that were with him were struck by the calmness with which he faced a decision on which so much depended. After weighing the alternative Eisenhower said that the real risk lay in the decision not to go. How right he was to approach the decision in that way is now clear to us in the light of our subsequent knowledge of events. The decision to go having been made, it so happened that the next suitable period (19 June and successive days) saw the worst June storms in living memory."

Overlord, the largest and most complex single military operation the world had ever seen, was on; and the Germans, because security about the Allied plans had been so well maintained, because the cover plan to deceive the enemy had been so cleverly executed, and because the weather did not seem suitable for an assault on the Normandy coast, were not expecting it. In fact, Field Marshal Rommel had left his headquarters on the

[1]B. T. Batsford Ltd., 1973.

morning of June 4 for a visit to Germany; and many of his senior officers were attending an exercise.

One of the Typhoon squadrons in the 2nd Tactical Air Force was No 164, based for *Overlord* operations at Thorney Island near Chichester, Sussex. Its operations record book notes that on June 5, 1944, all their aircraft had been given black-and-white distinctive markings (the stripes on fuselage and wings that distinguished the aircraft supporting the Normandy landings). On June 4, the ORB entry states, there was no flying; but on the 5th, "two morning attacks on radar targets at St Valery, strikes with cannon and R/P (rocket projectiles)". Then it adds, dramatically: "At last light two aircraft flew a recce of Cherbourg Peninsula and came back very excited, having seen in the Channel the great armadas of sea and air which mean the opening of the Western European Front".

At nearby RAF Tangmere the AOC No 11 Group, AVM H. Saunders, briefed his squadron commanders on what was to happen; the scene is vividly described in *Against the Sun,* by Edward Lanchbery[1], the story of Wg Cdr Roland Beamont who at the time commanded No 150 Wing (two Tempest squadrons and one of Spitfire IXs):-

"The animated buzz of conversation hushed suddenly as the Air Officer Commanding, Air Vice-Marshal Saunders, entered the Operations room. He waited whilst a sheaf of maps was unrolled and pinned to the blackboards. This was IT, right enough. Red, blue, yellow and black lines stretched across the maps from London, Dungeness, Portsmouth, Southampton and the West Country, to a point south of the Isle of Wight, and then on across the Channel to Normandy.

"There was no need to command attention. Every man waited upon the AOC in eager anticipation.

" 'Gentlemen,' he said, 'tomorrow is D-day. I will outline briefly the plan as it concerns us, and then I wish you to return to your units to open and study your sealed orders for Operation *Overlord*. You will brief your wings at dusk and be instantly available from midnight onwards.

"The armies have already been safely embarked and are at this moment moving out for the concentration point off the Isle of Wight. By midnight they will be forming up a few miles off shore for the landing between Caen and Bayeux. From midnight onwards airborne landings, culminating in the landing of a large glider force at 0400 hours, will take place throughout the area in preparation for the main assault.

"For our part the Tactical Air Force will supply close support to the army on a scale which will keep every one of their aircraft constantly in the air. In addition the RAF and USAAF will maintain a continuous patrol of two hundred fighters over the beaches from thirty minutes before sunrise until thirty minutes after sunset. With the force available this means four patrols a day for each squadron. It is a heavy responsibility, and the first four days will be extremely hard work, but after that we can expect to revert to a less rigorous programme.

" 'The enemy is not expected to react in the air in great numbers on the first day, but may appear in force up to two or three hundred strong in three or four days. That will be your opportunity.

[1]Cassell & Co, 1955.

Arming the RAF fighter-bombers:-

Belting-up cannon-shells for Spitfire IXs. In the background can be seen (from left) aircraft of Nos 411 (coded DB-), 56 (US-) and – just visible – 332 (AH-) Squadrons

Rockets from Typhoons, showing the fins which gave directional stability after launching, and the 60lb explosive head. In the background, a Typhoon Ib of No 609 Sqn

"Not a man had less than three decorations . . .": in this group are two of the most distinguished RAF fighter pilots, Group Captain A. G. ('Sailor') Malan, DSO, DFC, *from South Africa (second from left) and Wing Commander W. V. Crawford-Compton,* DSO, DFC, *from New Zealand (right)*

" 'Finally, gentlemen,' concluded the AOC, 'I need hardly remind your that the Royal Air Force has never failed in a mission. Many of you took part, years ago, in incredible victories against tremendous odds:[1] victories which set a standard that has been maintained ever since. You are now on the brink of the greatest adventure of all, and I have no doubt as to the outcome of your part in it. ...'"

At 0020 hours on June 6, 1944, the first parachutists, vanguard of Operation *Overlord,* fell silently through the dark Normandy skies; the gliders released and sank towards a terrain they could not see until they were committed to landing on it. In the St Mère l'Eglise area of the Cherbourg Peninsula, inland from *Utah* Beach, about 920 C-47s/53s

---

[1]An earlier paragraph describes how Beamont "flew his Tempest, 'RB', shining in its new black-and-white, to Tangmere" for the briefing. "Parked outside the watch-office were Spitfire IX, XIIs and XIVs, Typhoons with bomb-racks and rocket projectile rails, and Mustangs, all bearing the initials of their owners. Top-scoring pilots Johnny Johnson, Peter Simpson, Don Kingaby, Hawkeye Wells, Jamie Jamieson, Scotty Scott, Johnny Baldwin, Jamie Rankin, Johnny Walker, Sailor Malan, Robin Johnston and Charles Green were but a few of them, wing leaders and sector commanders, veterans of the Battles of France and Britain. Not a man had less than three decorations. ..." There had been a similar scene at RAF Milfield, Northumberland, when fighter leaders' courses were held from February 1944 to train for the invasion. In *Tale of a Guinea Pig The Exploits of a World War II Fighter Pilot* by Geoffrey Page, DSO, DFC (Pelham Books, 1982), the author, newly appointed to command No 132 Squadron, describes how in the Mess "a milling throng of cheerful young men ... despite their apparent youth sported the ranks of squadron leaders and wing commanders combined with decorations for gallantry. ..."

Waco gliders towed to Normandy by C-47s of the USAAF IX Troop Carrier Command in the daisy-strewn field where they landed

Invasion arrival: tank-carrying General Aircraft Hamilcars, biggest gliders used by the Allies in Operation Overlord, about to touch down in Normandy on 6 June 1944

of the USAAF IXth Troop Carrier Command dropped the US Army 82nd and 101st Divisions and released about 100 Waco gliders during the next three hours. Unfortunately the landings were widespread owing to navigational errors, width of aircraft formation, and inexperience; but the American airborne troops achieved a significant measure of surprise, and despite losses of equipment cut the Germans' communications and disorganised their defences. On the left flank the British 6th Airborne Division were put down on ground between the River Dives and Orne, inland from what was to become *Sword* Beach, by about 360 aircraft and 96 gliders. The conveying or towing aircraft—Dakotas, Stirlings, Albermarles and Halifaxes—came from Nos 38 and 46 Groups. The very first landing in Normandy—at 0020 hours—seems to have been achieved by six Horsa gliders, towed by Halifaxes, carrying six platoons of the 2nd Battalion of the Oxford and Buckinghamshire Light Infantry plus a detachment of Royal Engineers. Their objective was to seize two bridges, over the Caen Canal (a swing bridge) and the River Orne. The gliders were released once the coast had been crossed, so that they would make a silent arrival, and four of them landed with great accuracy—one of them, PF800, touching-down within 47 yards of the swing bridge. A fifth landed half a mile away and the sixth on a bridge over the River Dives, some seven miles away. As with the Americans, the British airborne forces achieved their objectives after initial confusion and losses, largely resulting from the same causes, such as faulty navigation and a high wind, which caused a widespread drop and many casualties and losses of equipment before any action started. On neither flank was there any appreciable enemy air opposition, but aircraft and gliders encountered ground fire, and consequent evasive action increased the inaccuracy of dropping, both in release height and location.

Meanwhile the great seaborne armada of more than 2,700 vessels—largest concentrated shipment of armed forces the world had ever seen—moved slowly across the Channel towards Normandy, given fighter cover by the distinctive twin-tailed P-38 Lightnings of the USAAF IXth Air Force. That the ships were immune from air attack throughout the night, and were able to begin discharging their troops and equipment without interference from the Luftwaffe, was considered to be the first victory for the Allied Air Forces since Operation *Overlord* moved into gear with the sailings from the south coast ports.

But before the Allied Armies struggled ashore to face, initially, the German 7th Army, with the 1st and the 19th behind it and the 15th to the East, the Allied Air Forces had drenched the beach defences with bombs, some 1,760 tons being dropped. Taking part in these coastal attacks, which provided as dramatic an example of close-support tactical bombing as any seen during the Second World War, were B-17 Flying Fortresses and B-24 Liberators of the USAAF 8th Air Force and B-26 Marauders of the 9th. The warships which followed up this aircraft assault with a sea-to-shore bombardment were protected from coastal retaliation by a smoke screen laid by RAF Boston squadrons of No 2 Group, 2nd Tactical Air Force. However, the combined effect of the naval bombardment (which started at about 0530hr) and the bombers' attack which had preceded it failed to destroy the coastal defences, because of the thickness of the concrete which covered the guns. Nor was the air bombing effective in all cases, because of bombs being dropped too far inland in order to avoid casualties to the Allied forces. The troops started to go ashore, in some 4,266 landing ships and craft, at about 0630 hours; and on *Omaha* beach the Americans found to their cost that the air and naval bombardments had had little effect. Further, the seas were rough, many boats and amphibious tanks sank offshore, and onshore the Germans were in much greater strength than had been anticipated; so the Americans had a bitter struggle to gain a foothold and suffered many casualties. On *Utah* beach things went much better, because of a successful preparatory attack by about 270 B-26 Marauders of the US 9th Air Force, bombing at heights of between 3,000ft and 7,000ft. At *Sword* beach the arrival of the assault boats immediately followed attacks by Typhoons, 12 squadrons of which had been ordered to attack strong points, defended localities or batteries on or near the beaches in the British area when the advance from the sea was made. At *Gold* beach the Typhoons failed to knock out their target on one flank, and progress inland was consequently held up; and at *Juno* beach the Canadian 3rd Division was late in arriving, so the defences had revived after the air assault; but an advance was made to the immediate objectives. The Allies had successfully stormed the ramparts of *Festung Europa.*

Air support for the landings:-

USAF 9th Air Force B-26s going in to precede the invasion forces with close-support tactical bombing

The D-day scene:-

Air-to-air and air-to-sea view of the Allied liberation of Europe, Operation Overlord, as the Halifaxes tow their Horsa gliders towards Normandy above the Allied shipping off the beaches

During the remainder of D-day the figher-bombers of the US 9th Air Force and RAF 2nd Tactical Air Force continued to give close support to the assault troops, either responding to requests or making armed reconnaissances in search of targets of opportunity. On this first day of Operation *Overlord,* little was seen of the Luftwaffe, largely because the Germans had been taken by surprise. Nevertheless the Allied Air Forces did not relax their vigilance in protecting the shipping lanes between the British and Normandy coasts: six groups of P-38 Lightnings from the US 8th and 9th Air Forces were given responsibility for protecting them by day, while aircraft of the RAF ADGB (Air Defence of Great Britain) and No 85 Group took over the night fighter role. The anchorages and beaches from five miles inland to 15 miles offshore were protected by a low cover of Spitfires and a higher cover of P-47 Thunderbolts. Further inland, P-51 Mustangs and P-38 Lightnings (the longer-endurance fighters) of the USAAF 8th Fighter Command flew area patrols to screen the battle zones from the rest of France. On D-day these fighters, making their patrols to surround Normandy and attacking targets at the end of them, operated during three periods from 0500hr onwards and completed nearly 2,000 sorties.

In two respects, however, the Allied air forces had debits to their accounts on D-day. Although losses of aircraft carrying the airborne force had been light, the losses of paratroops had been as heavy as the C-in-C Allied Expeditionary Air Force, Air Chief Marshal Sir Trafford Leigh-Mallory, had feared they would be; secondly, weather conditions militated against successful attacks by the Allied heavy bombers—nearly all of a force of more than 500 Liberators and Fortresses having to return on the second mission of D-day without bombing eight key centres in Normandy—and offset the overwhelming advantages of massive air superiority enjoyed by the Allies. However, during the night of D-day some 977 Lancasters and Halifaxes of RAF Bomber Command attacked nine centres, the intention being to block routes through the main towns of Normandy.

The Luftwaffe was not strong enough in France at the time of the Allied landings—Luftflotte 3 had fewer than 300 serviceable bombers and about 315 fighters—to make a significant response to them. Apart from the Allies' numerical air superiority, the element of surprise had left the Luftwaffe unprepared for retaliation. One fighter squadron, indeed, had been moved just before D-day except for two pilots; these, Oberst J. Priller and Sgt H. Wodarcsyk, flew over the Allied armada and shot up *Sword* beach in their FW190s.

Within 24 hours of the first landings being made, the Allies had gained a foothold in Europe from which they would not be dislodged: Operation *Overlord* had succeeded in its initial objective. It could not have done so, however, without Allied air superiority—gained in 1943 and never relinquished. Many severe battles lay ahead: establishment of ground superiority in Normandy; the break-out from the landing areas; the German missile counter-offensives; Arnhem; the Ardennes battle in December 1944; and the crossing of the Rhine. But in the end, with the Russians advancing from the east, the defeat of Nazi Germany was assured; and in that defeat, air power had played a significant part—not least in making it possible for the Allies to put their armies ashore on the hostile, highly defended coast of Normandy on June 6, 1944.

Appendix I

Directive to the Supreme Commander Allied Expeditionary Force

(Issued February the 12th, 1944)

1. You are hereby designated as Supreme Allied Commander of the forces placed under your orders for operations for the liberation of Europe from the Germans. Your title will be Supreme Commander, Allied Expeditionary Force.

2. *Task.* You will enter the Continent of Europe and, in conjunction with the other United Nations, undertake operations aimed at the heart of Germany and the destruction of her armed forces. The date for entering the Continent is the month of May, 1944. After adequate Channel ports have been secured, exploitation will be directed towards securing an area that will facilitate both ground and air operations against the enemy.

3. Notwithstanding the target date above, you will be prepared at any time to take immediate advantage of favourable circumstances, such as withdrawal by the enemy on your front, to effect a re-entry into the Continent with such forces as you have available at the time; a general plan for this operation when approved will be furnished for your assistance.

4. *Command.* You are responsible to the Combined Chiefs of Staff and will exercise command generally in accordance with the diagram at Appendix A (reproduced below). Direct communication with the United States and British Chiefs of Staff is authorized in the interest of facilitating your operations and for arranging necessary logistic support.

5. *Logistics.* In the United Kingdom the responsibility for logistics organization, concentration, movement and supply of forces to meet the requirements of your plan will rest with British Service Ministries so far as British Forces are concerned. So far as United States Forces are concerned, this responsibility will rest with the United States War and Navy Departments. You will be responsible for the co-ordination of logistical arrangements on the Continent. You will also be responsible for co-ordinating the requirements of British and United States Forces under your command.

6. *Co-ordination of operations of other Forces and Agencies.* In preparation for your assault on enemy-occupied Europe, sea and air forces, agencies of sabotage, subversion, and propaganda, acting under a variety of authorities, are now in action. You may recommend any variation in these activities which may seem to you desirable.

7. *Relationship to United Nations Forces in other areas.* Responsibility will rest with the Combined Chiefs of Staff for supplying information relating to operations of the forces of the USSR for your guidance in timing your operations. It is understood that the

Soviet forces will launch an offensive at about the same time as *Overlord* with the object of preventing the German forces from transferring from the Eastern to the Western front. The Allied Commander-in-Chief, Mediterranean Theatre, will conduct operations designed to assist your operation, including the launching of an attack against the south of France at about the same time as *Overlord*. The scope and timing of his operations will be decided by the Combined Chiefs of Staff. You will establish contact with him and submit to the Combined Chiefs of Staff your views and recommendations regarding operations from the Mediterranean in support of your attack from the United Kingdom. A copy of his directive is furnished for your guidance. The Combined Chiefs of Staff will place under your command the forces operating in Southern France as soon as you are in a position to assume such command. You will submit timely recommendations compatible with this regard.

8. *Relationship with Allied Governments–the re-establishment of Civil Governments and Liberated Allied Territories and the administration of enemy territories.* Further instructions will be issued to you on these subjects at a later date.

Appendix A

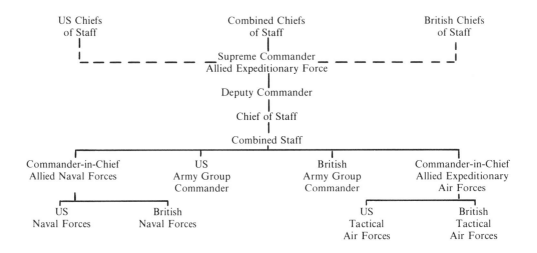

Appendix II

Luftwaffe Operational Commands

Combined High Command
(Oberkommando der Wehrmacht)

Luftwaffe High Command
(Oberkommando der Luftwaffe)

Luftflotte[1]   *Luftflotte*   *Luftflotte*   *Luftflotte*

Fliegerdivision[2]   *Fliegerdivision*

Geschwader[3]   *Geschwader*   *Geschwader*

Staff Flight   1st *Gruppe*[4]   IInd *Gruppe*   IIIrd *Gruppe*   IVth *Gruppe*

Staff Flight   1st *Staffel*[5]   2nd *Staffel*   3rd *Staffel*   4th *Staffel*

Notes:
(1) *Luftflotten,* numbered 1, 2, 3, 4 and 5, later 6 also. These were allocated to cover a set geographical area, and comprised all types of flying units; their strength could be anything between 200 and 1,300 aircraft, depending upon the importance of the area.
(2) The *Fliegerdivision,* later renamed *Fliegerkorps,* could operate either within or independent of a *Luftflotte.* It too comprised all types of flying units; its strength could be anywhere between 200 and 750 aircraft, depending upon the importance of its area.
(3) The *Geschwader* was the largest German formation to have a nominal fixed strength; it usually comprised 90 aircraft in three *Gruppen* plus a Staff Flight with four. Within a *Geschwader* the aircraft were normally confined to one role, i.e. *Jagdgeschwader* (JG)—fighters, *Nachtjagd-* (NJG)—night fighters, *Zerstoerer-* (ZG)—heavy fighters, *Kampf-* (KG)—bombers, *Stuka-* (StG)—dive bombers, *Schlacht-* (SG)—ground attack.
(4) A *Gruppe* usually comprised 27 aircraft in three *Staffeln,* and a Staff Flight with three. The IVth *Gruppe* was a training unit, attached to a bomber *Geschwader.*
(5) The *Staffel* comprised nine aircraft. Usually there were three *Staffeln* in a *Gruppe,* but sometimes a fourth was added.

Reproduced, by permission, from *Pictorial History of the Luftwaffe,* by Alfred Price; Ian Allan, 1969.

Glossary of Code Names

Crossbow	Allied measures against V-weapon sites.
Fortitude	Deception plan for *Overlord.*
Neptune	Naval assault phase of *Overlord.*
Overlord	Allied invasion of north-west Europe in 1944.
Pointblank	Combined Bomber Offensive against Germany.
Utah *Omaha*	Assault beaches, American sector
Gold *Juno* *Sword*	Assault beaches, British sector

Bibliography

OFFICIAL HISTORIES

The Army Air Forces in World War II, ed by W. F. Craven and J. L. Cate; University of Chicago Press, Vol II 1949, Vol III 1951. *The Defence of the United Kingdom,* by Basil Collier, HMSO, 1957. *History of the Second World War: The Mediterranean and the Middle East (Vol III),* by Maj-Gen I. S. O. Playfair, CB, DSO, MC, and *Grand Strategy* (Vol V), by John Ehrman; HMSO, 1960 and 1956; *Royal Air Force 1939-1945* by Hilary St George Saunders and Denis Richards; HMSO, 1954. *The Strategic Air Offensive against Germany,* Vols III and IV, by Sir Charles Webster and Noble Frankland; HMSO, 1961. *Victory in the West* by Maj L. F. Ellis; HMSO, 1962 and 1968. *SOE in France,* by M. R. D. Foot, HMSO, 1966. *Report by the Supreme Commander to the Combined Chiefs of Staff, on the Operations in Europe of the Allied Expeditionary Force;* HMSO, 1946.

AIR FORCE RECORDS

Second Report of the Commanding General of the US Army Air Forces to the Secretary of War; HMSO, 1945. *Ninth Air Force April-Nov 1944,* [US] Army Air Forces Historical Study No 36, Oct 1945. *The Rise and Fall of the German Air Force, (1933 to 1945);* the Air Ministry, 1948. Public Record Office documents:-

Air 40/1645	Tabular record of German Air Force activity against UK, 1941-1944
Air 40/1646-9	Enemy air activity over British Isles, 1942-1944.
Air 40/1653	Location of enemy activity over UK, 1941-1945
Air 25/23	Operations Record Book, No 2 Group, 1941-3
Air 25/24	Operations Record Book, No 2 Group, 1944
Air 25/28	Operations Record Book, Allied Expeditionary Air Force, 1943-4
Air 25/586	Operations Record Book, No 38 Group, 1943-May '45
Air 25/588	Operations Record Book, No 38 Group, Appendices, Sept 1943-June 1944
Air 25/777	Operations Record Book, No 100 Group, 1943-5.

HISTORIES

The Second World War 1939-45, by Maj-Gen J. F. C. Fuller; Eyre and Spottiswoode, 1948. *Overture to Overlord,* by Lt-Gen Sir Frederick Morgan, KCB; Hodder & Stoughton, 1950. *The Struggle for Europe,* by Chester Wilmot; Collins, 1952. *The United States and World War II, Vol II,* by A. Russell Buchanan, Harper & Row, 1964. *The Great Battles of World War II,* by Henry Maule, Hamlyn, 1973. *Triumph in the West 1943-1946,* by Arthur Bryant; Collins, 1959. *Inside the Third Reich,* by Albert Speer; Weidenfeld and Nicholson, 1970.

AUTOBIOGRAPHIES AND BIOGRAPHIES

Against the Sun The Story of Wg Cdr Roland Beamont, DSO, OBE, DFC, by Edward Lanchbery; Cassell & Co Ltd, 1955. *Bomber Commander The Life of James H. Doolittle,* by Lowell Thomas and Edward Jablonski; Sidgwick & Jackson Ltd, 1977. *Mission Completed,* by Air Chief Marshal Sir Basil Embry; Methuen & Co, 1957. *Rommel,* by Desmond Young; Collins, 1950. *The First and the Last,* by Adolph Galland; Methuen, 1955. *With Prejudice,* by Marshal of the RAF Lord Tedder; Cassell & Co Ltd, 1966. *Eisenhower as Military Commander,* by Maj-Gen E. K. G. Sixsmith; B. T. Batsford Ltd, 1973. *Eisenhower was my boss,* by Kay Summersby; T. Werner Laurie Ltd, 1949. *The Rise and Fall of the Luftwaffe The Life of Luftwaffe Marshal Erhard Milch,* by David Irving; Weidenfeld and Nicholson, 1973. *Tale of a Guinea Pig The Exploits of a World War II Fighter Pilot,* by Geoffrey Page, DSO, DFC; Pelham Books, 1982. *German Commanders of World War II,* by Anthony Kemp; Osprey Publishing Ltd, 1982.

AIR FORCE HISTORIES

Bomber Squadrons of the RAF, by P. J. R. Moyes; Macdonald & Co, 1964. *Confound and Destroy, 100 Group and the Bomber Support Campaign,* by M. Streetly; Macdonald & Jane's, 1978. *The German Air Force,* by Wg Cdr A. Lee; Duckworth, 1946. *The Luftwaffe a History,* by J. Killen; F. Muller, 1967. *The Luftwaffe at War, 1939-45,* by A. Galland, K. Ries and R. Ahnert; Ian Allan, 1972. *Pictorial History of the Luftwaffe,* by Alfred Price; Ian Allan, 1969. *Pictorial History of the RAF* (Vol 2), by John W. R. Taylor and Philip J. R. Moyes; Ian Allan, 1969. *Pictorial History of the USAF,* by David Mondey; Ian Allan, 1969. *The Royal Air Force and USAAF from July 1943 to September 1944* (Britain at War series), by Air Cdre L. E. O. Charlton; Hutchinson, 1946. *No 83 Group 1943/45,* by Sqn Ldr D. R. Morgan; 1957. *The Luftwaffe War Diaries,* by Cajus Bekker; Macdonald & Co (Publishers) Ltd, 1967. *2nd Tactical Air Force,* by Christopher F. Shores; Osprey, 1970. *The Air Marshals,* by Allen Andrews; Macdonald & Co Ltd, 1970. *The 9th Air Force in World War II,* by Kenn C. Rust; Aero Publishers Inc, 1967. *Die Ritter Kreuz Träger der Luftwaffe, 1939-1945, B and 1 Jagdflieger,* by Ernst Obermaier; verlag Dieter Hoffman, Mainz, 1966.

STRATEGY AND TACTICS

Air Power in War, by A. H. Narracott; Frederick Muller, 1945. *Air Power in War,* by Lord Tedder; Hodder and Stoughton, 1948. *Full Circle The Story of Air Fighting,* by AVM J. E. ('Johnnie') Johnson; Chatto and Windus, 1964. *The Air Plan that Defeated Hitler,* by Maj-Gen Haywood S. Hansell Jr, USAF (Ret); Atlanta, Ga, 1972. *Aircraft versus Submarine,* by Alfred Price; William Kimber, 1973. *Instruments of Darkness,* by Alfred Price; William Kimber, 1967. *Photo Reconnaissance – The Operational History,* by Andrew J. Brookes; Ian Allan, 1975. *World War II Photo Intelligence,* by Col Roy M. Stanley II, USAF; Sidgwick & Jackson, 1982.

AIRBORNE FORCES

By Air to Battle The Official Account of the British First and Sixth Airborne Divisions; HMSO, 1945. *Currahee! 'We Stand Alone' A paratrooper's account of the Normandy Invasion,* by Donald Burgett; Hutchinson, 1967. *D-day with the Screaming Eagles,* by George E. Koskimaki; Vantage Press, 1970. *The Wooden Sword,* by Lawrence Wright; Elek Books Ltd, 1967. *Airborne to Battle: a History of Airborne Warfare 1918-1971,* by Col Maurice Tugwell; William Kimber, 1971. *The Big Drop The Guns of Merville, June 1944,* by John Golley; Jane's, 1982.

CAMPAIGN ACCOUNTS

The Battle of the V-weapons, 1944-45, by Basil Collier; Hodder & Stoughton Ltd, 1964. *The Longest Day June 6, 1944,* by Cornelius Ryan; Victor Gollancz, 1960. *D-Day,* by Warren Tute/John Costello & Terry Hughes; Sidgwick & Jackson, 1974. *Six Armies in Normandy,* by John Keegan; Jonathan Cape, 1982.

AIRCRAFT

Aircraft of World War II, by Kenneth Munson; Ian Allan, 1972. *The Mosquito,* by C. Martin Sharp and M. J. F. Bowyer, Faber & Faber, 1967.

PHOTOGRAPHIC ACKNOWLEDGEMENTS

Imperial War Museum: 13, 20, 32, 39 *bottom,* 40 *bottom,* 57, 61, 62, 65 *bottom,* 68, 78, 99, 100, 107, 108, 109, 110, 111, 118, 120, 128, 129 *top,* 129 *bottom,* 131, 132, 133, 134, 137.
US Air Force: 23, 24, 35 *top,* 35 *bottom,* 43, 74, 80.
Philip Moyes: 39 *top, middle,* 40 *top.*
Bundesarchiv: 49, 50, 51, 52, 53.
Ministry of Defence: 65 *top.*
Chas Bowyer: 93, 94
H. Holmes: 103.

Index